SEE NO EVIL
SPEAK NO EVIL

A HISTORY OF MOB VIOLENCE
IN THE TEXAS HEARTLAND
1869-1904

by
Ross McSwain

ISBN
0-9789601-7-3 (10 digit)
978-0-9789601-7-9 (13 digit)

Library of Congress Control Number: 2008940641

First Edition

Printed in the United States of America
Published by Shadetree Enterprises
2536 Princeton Ave.
San Angelo, TX 76904-5845
(325) 949-6180

Table of Contents

Foreword

Scholars trying to trace the history of the West have often been stymied when they attempt to learn the facts about the specific acts of violence. Though most of these incidents have receded more than a century into the past, families of both victims and perpetrators were reluctant or afraid to talk about them at the time. As years went on and those with first-hand knowledge passed away, much of the truth was buried with them. Today the historian has to find what he can in old legal records, and sort through as best he can the sometimes contradictory accounts that have been handed down as family folklore. Now and then he is fortunate enough to find notes and memoirs written long ago by those who knew.

Mostly, however, the details are lost in the dust of time, and one is left to ponder how much to believe of folklore and legend.

One area in which much mystery remains is that of mob violence, rampant in several Central Texas counties from the end of the Civil War to about the turn of the century. For decades it laid a blanket of fear over the people, for even to talk about it was to tempt death. The movement usually was started by prominent citizens as an extra-legal way to punish cattle and horse thieves, robbers, and murderers when law enforcement was broken down, intimidated, or in many cases implicated. In time, however, these mob actions almost always became corrupted, falling under control of people whose agendas had little to do with enforcing the law but much to do with breaking it.

Ross McSwain has brought together as many of the facts about the mob as can be found a century or more after the incidents had occurred. What he has uncovered is a startling view of Texas at its wildest and most violent, a time when hardened men thought no more of cold-blooded murder than of blowing out a lamp. It is a sad truth that many of these crimes went unpunished except, in some cases, by a reciprocal murder.

For those who believe Old West violence is sometimes exaggerated, check the mob's body count.

Elmer Kelton

Acknowledgements

Some 40 years ago, while covering farm and ranch news for the *San Angelo Standard-Times*, a daily West Texas newspaper, I had an evening visit with the late Lucius M. "Mick" Stephens, a Lometa wool and mohair merchant. Mr. Stephens had a keen interest in Central Texas history, and was the first person to tell me about mob violence that thrived in the Texas Heartland after the Civil War. He gave me a copy of C. L. Sonnichsen's book, *I'll Die Before I Run,"* which featured a chapter on the San Saba Mob, along with other stories about various Texas feuds. The story drew my interest because I grew up in adjoining McCulloch County and had never heard of this bloody period of time.

Some years later, while having breakfast in Fort Worth with another friend, the late Casey Heatherly, a San Saba County rancher and then president of the American Angus Association, the mob story again came up in conversation. He told me that his ranch was located near the area in which much of the mob action had taken place. We agreed to work together and try and find out some of the story details.

After a number of months of telephone conversations and correspondence, a rather dejected and disappointed Heatherly notified me that our research project should come to an end. "No one will talk about it," Heatherly said. "Perhaps it best we leave it alone."

The story came alive again many years later when I wrote in my weekly newspaper column "Out Yonder" about how another area – Mason County in the Texas Hill Country – had opened up its secrets of the Hoo-Doo War during a seminar arranged by the Mason County Historical Commission. I made the observation that San Saba County folks ought to discuss its mob history from the frontier days. Too much history has been forgotten because of folks being

3

unwilling to talk about the past.

The telephone started to jingle and e-mails started arriving with tips, stories about family involvement and suggestions on how to develop the story and where to find information. I soon learned that mob violence was not just limited to San Saba County, but could be found in some dozen counties in the Texas Heartland. Thus, this project grew in size and scope.

I started to really devote time to researching this story in 2003. My efforts were delayed somewhat in 2005 when I had to have another heart surgery. Since I was prohibited from doing any manual work, I spent many hours and days reading research materials. The project became one of the most difficult I have ever experienced.

In addition to my late friends, Mickey Stephens and Casey Heatherly, I am indebted to many, many others, including several who have passed away.

Special thanks go to my friend and mentor, Elmer Kelton, who wrote the foreword to this book and also encouraged me to get it completed, and to Felton Cochran, owner of Cactus Book Shop in San Angelo, who gave me assurance that the book would drew reader interest and would be salable. Also, Ginnie Bivona, my editor, and her colleagues at Lone Star Productions, whose expertise put the book into print.

Special thanks go to Nedra Stringfellow Magnan of Burnet, daughter of the late E.M. "Ned" Stringfellow, editor and publisher of the *Richland Springs Eye-Witness,* who shared with me pages and pages of her father's original notes he made while interviewing people for an anniversary edition of his newspaper published in 1953. Nedra, who served as a special correspondent for the *Standard-Times,* at one time planned to write a book about the mob violence that caused so much trouble in her home county.

Another who is due special thanks is San Saba County

Attorney David Williams, who has supported my efforts for several years. His research paper on the Brooks-Kendall-Brown courthouse shooting, presented several years ago to a meeting of the Edwards Plateau Historical Association annual meeting, was an important resource in preparing this story.

One of my most enduring friends, Frederica Wyatt of Junction, one of the Texas Hill Country's best historians and chair of the Kimble County Historical Commission, made available to me a copy of excerpts from the unpublished memoirs of Archie Douglas Hannah, pioneer settler on the Colorado River in Brown County and some other research materials. I am deeply grateful for this expression of friendship.

David Johnson, an Indiana resident who has had a longtime interest in Texas history and author of a book on the Mason County Hoo-Doo War, was especially thoughtful in providing me copies of the late C.L. Sonnichsen's handwritten notes which the noted historian made during interviews conducted in the 1940s while developing his book, *"I'll Die Before I Run."*

Also, I want to again thank my special friends, John and Nancy Bannister of San Saba, who offered me the use of their guesthouse at their ranch. It was a wonderful, quiet place to do research and rest. John, a retired military man, found on coming to San Saba that he carried the same name as one of the Texas Rangers who was sent to the area in the 1870s. However, he was never able to make a family connection with the frontier lawman.

Retired Texas Ranger Lieutenant Bob Favor, who served in the Central Texas area with Company F in Brady from 1969 to 1982, provided me with the Vogel story that had been told to him personally by the late McCulloch County Sheriff Luke Vogel. Bob Favor is a special friend.

Another special person who waded through this mass of words, looking for misspelled words, poor grammar and other glaring errors is retired San Angelo newspaper editor Perry Flippin, whose old grandfather, Isaac Milton Draper, recalled tales of mob violence in Williamson County. Mr. Draper's sister, Vi, married outlaw Bill Longley's brother, Jim.

It seems that the list is endless of folks who shared family stories, provided information from other sources or offered contacts that knew of stories from those brutal times. They include Jane Hoerster of Mason, chair of the Mason County Historical Commission, the late Jerry Ponder of Mason, former Mason County Sheriff Don Grote, Mark Langford of Lampasas, Comanche County Librarian Margaret Waring, Joy and Charles Blake of Brenham and Robert Lee, Nelda Weathersby of San Saba, John R. Herridge of San Angelo, Bob Green, Richey and Shirley Reed and Jan Moreland Laughlin, all of Goldthwaite, Judy Nickels of San Angelo and Fort Worth, Don Woodruff of San Saba, Mary Lou Harris of Fort Stockton, Gerald Watkins of Austin and Brady Johnson of San Angelo. Also, Mozelle Gray Tonne, Karen Gauny Crisalli and Laura E. Ethridge, whose resident addresses are unavailable.

Several institutions and their associates also provided assistance in providing materials and photographic images. These include Jim Bradshaw, archivist at the Nita Stewart Haley Memorial Library in Midland; Suzanne Campbell, Head, West Texas Collection at Angelo State University Porter Henderson Memorial Library, and her staff, Shannon Sturm, university archivist, and Carol Mathews, cataloging, WTC; Ellen K. Brown, Associate Director and Archivist, The Texas Collection at Baylor University, Waco, and her graduate assistant, Nicholas Pruitt of Plainview; Ellen Humphries Brisendine, Archivist, The Cattleman Magazine, Fort Worth; and Eloisa Rodriguez, Library assistant, Lampasas Public Library.

Supplying historical photo images from their personal collections were author-historian Mike Cox of Austin, and Jack Siscoe of Rayville, Louisiana. Mr. Siscoe provided a photo of

6

early-day San Saba County Sheriff Andrew Jackson Hawkins. Other images were provided by the *Livestock Weekly,* San Angelo, and photographer Bob Zeller, also of San Angelo. I have strived to catalog all the names of persons who helped provide me with various research materials, but I may have overlooked or forgotten someone. I hope that is not the case, but if so it was not intentional. Again, my sincere thanks to each of you.

Ross McSwain
August 30, 2008

Prologue

Prior to the 1880s, a vast area of Central Texas was outlaw country by unanimous consent. Because of the isolation of the area during and after the Civil War, this large region that encompassed some dozen counties became infested with desperate criminals: cattle rustlers, horse thieves, murderers, army deserters, carpetbaggers and jayhawkers. A few bands of Comanche and Kiowa Indians continued to raid in the area, carrying off captives, burning homes and stealing horses and mules.

Law enforcement was scant at best. In the few organized counties that existed then, sheriffs and constables were content to let these lawless people alone, as long as they did not overstep their bounds. The sheriffs thought it better "to isolate the disease than to scatter it," writes historian Flora Gatlin Bowles, editor of the book, *"A No Man's Land Becomes A County."*

Violence gripped Central Texas for decades, and from this fertile ground emerged some of the west's most deadly and picturesque gunmen, including Emmanuel "Mannen" Clements Sr., his brothers, Gyp, Jim and Joe, his son, Emmanuel "Mannie" Clements Jr., and later his son-in-law, Deacon Jim Miller, and Clements' cousin, John Wesley Hardin; Dee Harkey; John Calhoun Pinckney "Pink" Higgins; Tom Horrell and his brothers, Mart, Sam, Ben and Merritt; Tom "Black Jack" Ketchum; David Lyle Kemp; the Kilpatrick brothers and others.

These ruthless men left a trail of outlawry as they passed through Mills, San Saba, Brown, Llano, Hamilton, Lampasas and McCulloch counties, the heartland of Texas, stealing livestock, robbing banks and storekeepers, terrorizing settlers and killing lawmen and innocent citizens. Several served as lawmen, and they were as bad as the men they sought to arrest.

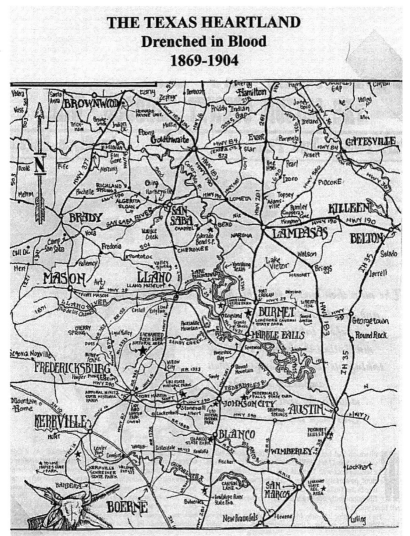

The Texas Heartland, 1869-1904, was a frontier battlefront after the Civil War. Map from the Ross McSwain collection.

In 1874, the government of Texas was returned to the people as Reconstruction ended in the South. However, lawlessness was rampant and conditions in Central Texas settlements were serious. Indians still were a threat, but there were worse elements gathering – a crime wave was on, reports historian Bowles.

As civil law vanished due to lax law enforcement, law-abiding citizens and community business leaders resorted to other methods of bringing law and order to their towns and counties. Vigilante committees were organized. Thus, organizations like the "Honest Man's Club," came into existence while at the same time opposing organizations like the "Trigger Mountain Mob" were formed.

Bowles writes that a violent hatred sprang up between these two groups. John M. Parks, a shrewd and brave individual was leader of the "Honest Man's" group. Dr. T. B. East was leader of the "Trigger Mountain" bunch. East was described as a man of mystery, but he made no secret of his distrust of persons about him.

East built a fortified house on a bluff on South Brown Creek in Mills County. He would meet all callers with a loaded rifle in his hands, even those coming to his home to ask for medical aide. Once he felt comfortable with the person, he would immediately fetch his doctor's satchel and go to the ill or injured party. When the mob problem subsided, East left Central Texas for the Indian Territory, now Oklahoma, where he was killed in the land rush.

While the Honest Man's Club was taking care of business – running rustlers and horse thieves out of the area – the Trigger Mountain bunch was also busy. Bowles says both groups had "good and bad" members, but when worthy members dropped out or were removed, they were replaced by men who had a private grudge against a neighbor, or desired his property. Revenge for some previous reason also resulted in murder.

The mob troubles began in 1869 near the Williams Ranch settlement and gradually grew worse. The vigilante committees first attempted to kill or run out of the country thieves and bad men who had settled there. Tragically, some innocent men were killed, and gradually it became a war of vengeance as friends and relatives of men killed organized to fight.

Historian-writer C. L. Sonnichsen, in his book, *"I'll Die Before I Run,"* wrote that the story of the Central Texas mobs and their activities "is not an easy one to tell, partly because so much of it was dark and mysterious, full of secret fears, midnight plottings, and unknown figures moving behind the scenes."

Sonnichsen spent years working on his book. He studied and researched 10 instances of extreme violence in Texas in the some 30 or more years following the Civil War. Sonnichsen notes that there were a number of mobs involved in so-called feuds in Central Texas, but the San Saba Mob was unique in that it was the only group that showed evidence of a formal organization with rituals.

According to Sonnichsen's findings, there were mobs, or vigilante groups in Coryell, Llano and Lampasas counties as well as those organized at Williams Ranch and other locations.

A number of years ago, my late friend, San Saba rancher Casey Heatherly and I met for breakfast at the Worth Hotel in Fort Worth, Texas. At the time I was regional editor for the *San Angelo Standard-Times,* a regional newspaper with circulation in Central and West Texas, and Casey was then serving as president of the American Angus Association, a national livestock organization. The Heatherly Ranch was located near a community where much of the violence occurred many years earlier.

Our conversation drifted to the San Saba Mob because one of the newspaper's special correspondents had submitted a story about that period of time and how the violence ended in the early 1900s.

"Yes," he said. He had heard stories about the mob and its ruthless activities, but knew little details of its existence. However, it was of historical interest to my friend and we

11

agreed to work together in gathering information about it. Months went by, and his letters brought little information. He was frustrated. No one was willing to talk about the mob's activities or possible family involvement. "Perhaps it is best to just forget about those days," he wrote.

On May 5, 2002, the Mason County Historical Commission sponsored a symposium on the Hoo-Doo War, a violent period of time in that county's history that correlated with mob activities in neighboring counties. I attended that symposium and another the following year and wrote a column about the various presentations. I casually mentioned that after four generations-plus, folks with knowledge of the San Saba Mob period should step forward and bring that historically important time into the open.

Within days after that column appeared, my telephone started to jingle with calls from people who had heard stories about the mob from family members. Soon, a significant number of messages arrived on my computer screen, adding additional information to a growing file.

This book is the result of many stories that have been shared with me by others, along with general research of newspaper reports, court records and other documents. Every effort has been made to provide factual information about a period of Texas history that has laid silent for too many years.

Ross McSwain
San Angelo, Texas

Chapter 1:
Why Were Mobs Formed?

"Wars breed crime and criminals, and the American Civil War did not differ from others in this respect. Out of the dislocations of that conflict grew a wave of lawlessness that transcended all expectations in the length of time it lasted, and in the number of successive generations in which it perpetuated itself as a noteworthy dynasty of outlawry," stated author Paul I. Wellman in his book, "*A Dynasty of Western Outlaws,*" published in 1961 by Doubleday and Company Inc. of New York.

Mob violence occurred in several counties of the Texas Heartland after the Civil War ended. Radical Republican rule, brought about by Reconstruction, resulted in the state having a lawless and chaotic environment.

A study conducted in 1869-70 by the Committee of Lawlessness and Violence of the Constitutional Convention, showed that the state was in dire need for a statewide organization that could work in any jurisdiction. The committee found that 939 murders had been committed between 1865 and 1868. Of these, 460 were committed by whites against whites, 373 involved whites murdering blacks, 10 were of blacks killing whites, and 57 were blacks slaying blacks. A later report showed an increase in murders during that same period totaling 1,035.

Sheriffs' reports from 1865 to 1871 revealed that 4,425 crimes were committed, but there were only 588 arrests and few convictions. The serious lack of justice was attributed to poor law enforcement, including the fact that only 82 counties had jails, of which many were so insecure that escapes were easily accomplished.

As a result of these numbers and reports of lawlessness,

13

the legislature passed the Police Act of July 1870 which authorized a force of 257 State Policemen, but the force never numbered more than 200. Under the act State Police could arrest offenders when local lawmen failed to do so. Adjutant General James Davidson was appointed chief of the State Police, and his force came from all walks of life, including some blacks, Hispanics, whites and veterans of both the Confederate and Union armies. Some – though few – were excellent lawmen. Others were criminals.

In December 1869 the police force totaled 196. By January 1872, it had dropped to 166 but later totaled 184 in January 1873. During the first month of operation, State Police made 978 arrests, including 109 for murder and 130 for attempted murder.

Despite the early success of the State Police, the fact that the force employed blacks and was controlled by Governor Edmund J. Davis made it extremely unpopular with citizens. Captain Jack Helm, one of the commanders, was accused of murdering prisoners. He was fired and later a warrant was issued for his arrest. Adjutant General Davidson embezzled more than $35,000 and disappeared. However, his crime cannot be blamed on the police.[1]

On April 22, 1873, the law that authorized the State Police was repealed. Captain Leander H. McNelly and some 36 other State Police officers became Texas Rangers. Although older studies indicate that the State Police were politically oriented and corrupt, evidence now does not support the charge.[2]

As in many sections of Central Texas, the outbreak of the war saw the banding together in Burnet County and other locations groups of lawless secessionists, who ruthlessly murdered and robbed citizens who were opposed to secession.

Among the first victims of this violence in Burnet County was John Scott, the county's first chief justice, or county judge, and two others, a man named McMasters and John R. Hubbard.

The men were victims of some "bushwhackers," according to historian Darrell Debo in his book, *Burnet County History, Volume I.*

Debo says a man named George A. Holland, the first white child born in the county, left a graphic account of the "bushwhackers" carried out against Union sympathizers. Holland states that many of the county's best men fled to Mexico or California. Scott, who had made a lot of money in the California goldfields, was cautioned by friends that he was a target of the band and should leave for Mexico. Secreting some $2,000 around his waist, Scott bid goodbye to his family and rode about seven miles to the home of a friend where he spent the night. The next morning, joined by McMasters, they left for a Colorado River crossing between Marble Falls and the community of Smithwick. Bushwhackers stopped them, robbed them, shot Scott to death and hanged McMasters. Their bodies were taken away several miles to "Dead Man's Hole," a 300-foot deep fracture, or fissure, in the rock. Scott's remains were recovered after the war. His wife identified the remains by a peculiar jawbone and teeth.[3]

Because of the distance from the main battlefronts of the war, Burnet and other neighboring counties in Central Texas escaped the ravages of the fight and the destruction that goes with bombardment. Even though the citizens escaped certain hardships and suffering, they did not escape the constant menace of Indian attacks, outlaws, rustlers and horse thieves.

Following Lee's surrender, Texas and other states of the Confederacy were put under military rule. Edmund J. Davis, a tyrannical public official, was named military governor. Federal troops were sent into the area to roundup Indians, deserters and bushwhackers, but a number of secessionists were caught up in the raids.

For a period of time from 1865 to 1876, criminals and cow thieves literally controlled the county. These outlaws were so bold that they threatened the court and many were turned loose. A conviction was very difficult to achieve during this period because witnesses and other respected citizens refused to appear in court and testify. Historian Debo says matters got so bad that a rancher could scarcely turn his cattle out in the pasture and expect to find them again.[4]

During 1868, Indians were extremely active raiding settlements and ranches from the Red River to the Rio Grande. Pioneers gathered in almost every locality to figure ways of protecting their lives, homes and property. Indians were not the only worry these hardy folks had to consider.

In Llano and Burnet counties, citizens had another threat. A so-called military company was raised under the commission of Governor Pease. This company of men was to aid the civil government in arresting and bringing to justice criminals who, they claimed, committed crimes during the Civil War. However, many members of the company were men who joined for the purpose of taking revenge on neighbors or others or for plunder. Many citizens were frightened of this band and refused to be taken under arrest, choosing instead to arm themselves and take off for the hills and brush to protect themselves. Matters had become desperate when settlers not only had to protect themselves from hostile Indians but also from white marauders.[5]

A settler in northern Burnet County, near the Lampasas County line, related that ranchers in the immediate area were losing livestock to a "single" Indian. A group of men chased the culprit out of the county. He was killed later and it was discovered that the man was not an Indian, but a white man dressed like an Indian.

The situation became so bad that Judge Emanuel Sampson refused to hold court in Burnet County unless the court was protected against violence and from threats of the lawless element. It was in just this kind of atmosphere that the county's first courthouse was burned on April 10, 1874, allegedly by arsonists. Since this was the time when cow thieves were the most active, it is noteworthy to remember that the cattle brands and marking records were destroyed in the fire.[6]

Similar problems were developing in neighboring Lampasas County. In fact, much of the violence was centered around a family in which five brothers were known to have short tempers and well-used six-shooters.

The 1870s were the most lawless years in Lampasas County history, reports writer Jeffrey Jackson who wrote about Central Texas lawlessness for the historical book, *"Lampasas County, Texas, Its History and Its People,"* published by the Lampasas County Historical Commission.

The town of Lampasas at the time was wide open where law and order was overpowered by outlaws and desperados in the county. There were numerous saloons for cowboys and others to get "lickered up," and plenty of doors and windows for targets. Jackson says the office of the local newspaper had all its windows shot out, and there were more than 20 bullet holes in the door of the law office of Gibson and White.

One of the favorite drinking establishments of the five Horrell brothers – Sam, Mart, Tom, Ben and Merritt – was Jerry Scott's Saloon, who advertised to having only the best cigars, whiskey, wine and brandy. Some major trouble brewed there on January 14, 1873, during the noon recess of District Court.

Sheriff S. T. Denson was attracted to loud voices and yelling coming from the saloon. The Short brothers – G. W. (Wash) and Mark – were having a whooping time and were disturbing the peace. When Denson attempted to arrest Wash Short, he resisted. While struggling, Mark got involved in the fracas and Wash was able to draw his pistol. He shot Denson once and attempted to shoot the sheriff again when a physician was able to get Denson out of the way.

The Shorts soon were on their way out of town with a posse in hot pursuit. At this time, the matter really got serious

17

when the Horrell brothers stopped the four men with drawn pistols, informed the posse leader Tom Sparks that they were friends of the Shorts and meant to protect them.

As a result of this shooting and confrontation, a group of citizens petitioned the governor for State Police to bring order to the community and for a law prohibiting the wearing of sidearms in Lampasas. This proclamation was approved and posted on February 10, 1873. Unfortunately, these measures only increased the violence in days and weeks to come.

On February 17, 1873, State Police Sergeant J. M. Redman arrived in Lampasas and posted the governor's proclamation prohibiting the wearing of firearms. During his stay, Redman did not make any arrests because no one was willing to testify against the lawless elements in the county. There were nighttime shootings, but Redman was unable to learn the shooters' identity. He returned to Austin on February 28, and told his superiors that law-abiding citizens there felt a need for police to be stationed there and for men to be allowed to carry firearms when the police force left.

On March 14, 1873, State Police Captain T. G. Williams and seven men arrived in Lampasas to help local authorities arrest persons charged with the attempted murder of Sheriff Denson. Before arriving in Lampasas, Williams and his men had met several freighters traveling to Austin. One of the teamsters, John Means, said the police captain had been drinking and told him he was going to clean up "those damned Horrell boys."[7]

A short time after arriving in Lampasas, Williams and his state policemen made their first arrest, charging Bill Bowen with carrying a six-shooter. Bowen, under some pretense, got Williams to enter Jerry Scott's Saloon, a favorite hangout of the Horrell bunch. Accompanied by officers J. M. Daniels, Wesley Cherry and Andrew Melville, Williams entered the drinking parlor and apparently got into an argument with Mart Horrell who claimed that Bowen, his brother-in-law, did not do

18

anything wrong and should not be arrested. Williams shot Mart Horrell, wounding him seriously. Before the smoke cleared the Horrells and their friends began firing at the police, killing Williams, Daniel and Cherry instantly. Melville, mortally wounded, died a few days later at the Huling Hotel.[8]

The barroom gunfight quickly moved into the street where Williams' other officers sought cover. One policeman, the only black present, mounted a fast horse and hurried back to Austin with the news. Tom Horrell also was wounded in the scrape, but not as seriously as his brother, Mart. After taking Mart to the home of his mother, the others quickly fled.

On March 20, 1873, an inquest was held over the deaths of the police. The coroner's jury found Tom Horrell, Martin Horrell, Merritt Horrell, Ben Turner, Joe Bolden, Allen Whitcraft, James Grizzell, Jerry Scott, Bill Bowen and Bill Gray responsible for the deaths of the police officers.

The state's top policeman, Frank Britton, then Adjutant General and Chief of Police, came to Lampasas with a dozen men to take charge of the investigation and to direct efforts in finding the accused men. Several different search groups were organized, including a sheriff's posse of citizens, a detachment of Burnet County Minute Men, and Britton's state police. A five-day search was carried out for the outlaws in Lampasas, Burnet, Llano, Coryell and Williamson counties.

The massive manhunt resulted in the arrest of Martin Horrell, Jerry Scott, Allen Whitcraft and James Grizzell. The men were taken to the Travis County jail in Austin. The governor's office offered a $3,000 reward, or $500 apiece, for the capture and arrest of the remaining men still at large.

Mart Horrell and the other prisoners were later transferred to the Williamson County jail in Georgetown, and Mart's wife was allowed to stay at the jail and care for his wounds suffered in the saloon shootout. When he was well enough to ride, she told his brothers.

On May 2, 1873, the Horrells made an attack on the

19

Georgetown jail and released the prisoners. A deputy sheriff and a man identified as a Mr. Fisher were wounded in the jailbreak. Meanwhile, the Horrells returned to Lampasas County where they had ranching operations. The Horrells had become such a ruthless and formidable force no one was willing to interfere with them or bring charges or complaints against them. According to historian Jackson, the men rode openly and made no effort to hide from lawmen and came to town whenever they pleased. When the brothers decided to relocate their cattle to New Mexico territory, they gathered the herd and notified the sheriff, S. T. Denson, when the herd would pass through Russell Gap in the event he wished to detain them. The sheriff chose to let the bunch pass without fanfare.[9]

Lampasas and Central Texas had not heard the last of the Horrells. They would create havoc during their short stay in New Mexico as well. On December 1, 1873, Ben Horrell and several others were killed while on a "spree" in Lincoln. This event started the "Horrell War" in New Mexico territory, a conflict between the local Mexican population, the Horrell brothers and their friends. The so-called war lasted about three months and cost the lives of some 37 men, mostly Mexicans. It was one of the most violent times in that section of the southwest and is possibly the prelude to the Lincoln County War that started sometime later.

Having now outlawed themselves in the New Mexico territory, the Horrells returned to Texas and Lampasas County. The state of Texas was now under a civil government with a newly elected governor, Richard Coke. Friends of the Horrells advised them to surrender and to stand trial for the killing of Captain Williams and his state policemen. The Horrells were assured by their friends that they would get a fair trial by Lampasas' best citizens. The men did turn themselves in, were tried and were acquitted of the charges.[10]

The Horrell brothers had not been free very long before

Merritt, the youngest, was accused by John Calhoun Pinckney "Pink" Higgins, a neighboring rancher, of unlawfully handling his cattle. A short time later, while Merritt, unarmed, was sitting in a chair of the old Jerry Scott Saloon, Higgins came in a back door of the bar and shot him to death.

Merritt's older brothers, Martin and Tom, were living on Sulphur Creek. The news of Merritt's killing was quickly delivered to the men and they headed for town. Pink Higgins and some friends had anticipated the Horrells would come into town ready for a fight. They stopped the Horrells on the outside of town and ambushed them. Tom Horrell's horse was killed in the gunfire and Mart Horrell was badly wounded. Tom Horrell, an experienced gunhand, fought off the attackers and helped carry his injured brother to a neighbor's house where a doctor was summoned.

Lampasas County quickly found itself in the middle of a classic family feud with Mart, Tom and Sam Horrell, Bill and Tom Bowen, John Dixon and Bill Crabtree on one side and Pink Higgins, Bob Mitchell and their friends on the other. The two factions met in town. One man was killed on each side and the population was greatly endangered.[11]

Texas Ranger John B. Jones, commander of the Frontier Battalion, was ordered by Governor Coke to send rangers to Lampasas to help quell the trouble. When Sergeant N. O. Reynolds reported to the sheriff, he learned that the Horrell boys were living on a ranch 10 miles east of Lampasas. Reynolds was told that from 10 to 12 desperate men were with the Horrells and it would be suicide to try and capture them. Reynolds, accompanied by a guide, arrived at the ranch after midnight. He and his men quietly entered the house. The Horrells were awakened with muzzles of pistols pointed at their faces. Reynolds assured the boys they would be treated fairly and be given a fair trial if they surrendered without a fight. He also assured the men they would be put in a jail where they could not be mobbed.

21

None of the Higgins gang was involved in the capture of the Horrells. They learned about it the next day and also quickly surrendered to the rangers.

After the arrest, the Horrells surprised everyone when they wrote a conciliatory letter to the Higgins bunch, which was quickly answered in a gentlemanly fashion. Copies of the letters appeared in the *Lampasas Dispatch* on Thursday, August 9, 1877. In brief, the Horrells told the Higgins that they "were honor bound to lay down our arms and to end the strife in which we have been engaged against you and exert our utmost efforts to eradicate all enmity from the minds of our friends who have sided with us in the troubles here in before alluded to. We promise furthermore to abstain from insulting or injuring you and your friends, to bury the bitter past forever, and to join with you as good citizens."[12]

In responding to the letter, Higgins, Robert Mitchell and William Wren noted that "we have carefully noted its contents and have approved most sincerely the spirit of communication…we will make every effort to do our part to restore good feelings and we lay down our weapons with our honest purpose to regard our former difficulties as bygone things, and we will urge our friends to do the same."[13]

Thus, the feud ended with this truce and even though some of the descendants of both families still reside in the vicinity, the unusual frontier peace treaty remained strong.

Sadly, violence that spread along each side of the Colorado River in the neighboring counties of Mills, San Saba, Brown and McCulloch could not be stopped by such a treaty. Mob justice was to take its toll on both the criminal element as well as innocent settlers and their families.

---

[1] "State Police," The Handbook of Texas Online,
   <http://www.tshaonline.org/handbook/online/>

[2] Ibid.

[3] Darrell Debo, <u>Burnet County History, Volume 1</u>, (Burnet, TX: Burnet County Historical Commission, 1979) p. 36.

[4] Ibid.

[5] Ibid.

[6] Ibid.

[7] John Clardy et al, <u>Lampasas County, Texas - Its History and Its People</u>, (Marceline, MO: Walsworth Publishing, 1991) p. 24.

[8] Ibid.

[9] Ibid.

[10] Jonnie Ross Elzner, <u>Relighting lamplights of Lampasas County, Texas</u>, (Hillsboro, TX: Hill Country Press, 1974).

[11] Ibid.

[12] Ibid.

[13] Ibid.

Chapter 2:
Where Did It Start?

The once prosperous community of Williams Ranch, located in Mills County, Texas, is now a ghost town just off U.S. Highways 84 and 183. In its heyday, Williams Ranch was three miles south of present Mullin, and eight miles northwest of Goldthwaite in central Mills County. However, when it was first organized in 1855, around a spring in the center of the John Williams ranch, the site was in present day Brown County.

According to the Handbook of Texas, the community was a major stop on a stage line between Austin and Brownwood, and it was a roundup point for cattle drives. Within a decade after the settlement was created, the community had several stores, a hotel, mill, a blacksmith shop and several saloons. The town got its post office in 1877. Along with its legitimate businessmen, ranchers and shopkeepers, it also was a hangout for all sorts of desperate men, including cattle rustlers, horse thieves, deserters from the Confederate army, jayhawkers (a member of the irregular bands that fought on either side during the Civil War), gamblers and other unsavory characters.

Texas was a haven for hundreds of unsavory characters immediately following the Civil War. Many of these people were deserters from both armies, particularly bloodied veterans from the rebel South.

While researching family data located in the University of Southern Mississippi library at Hattiesburg, my cousin, Robert J. McSwain of Petal, Mississippi, found several references to Confederate Army deserters making raids on their own neighbors, stealing livestock, burning crops, assaulting women and doing other unthinkable acts against poor and disadvantaged people in and around Augusta, Mississippi, in

Perry County. This band of raiders, led by Captain Newt Knight, was organized much like a cavalry unit with sub-officers and sergeants. These men, numbering about 75 or more, came from neighboring Jones County, Mississippi. A woman author, Ethel Knight, wrote a book titled *"Echo of the Black Horn – The Free State of Jones,"* that gave details of some of these raids. When the war ended with Lee's surrender, many of these kinds of men fled the South for new territory. Texas was the most inviting because it did not have much law enforcement and there was plenty of land available for homesteading.

During the settlement's peak years, 1877 to 1892, the area was headquarters for a number of West Texas cattlemen who held many conferences there. Eventually, telephone and telegraph lines passed through Williams Ranch from Austin to San Angelo. Several reasons for the demise of the town was the failure of the railroad passing through and strong disagreements between old and new residents. This led, in some instances, to bloodshed.

All that remains of Williams Ranch today is its cemetery. Among those buried there are John Williams, who gave the place its name; C. K. Conner; John Morris, a veteran who served in the 27th Brigade, Texas Militia, during the Civil War, who was killed by Indians; a former slave owned by Welcome Chandler named Albert, who was killed by a horse; and a man named N. A. Anthony, whose marker says he was "killed by the mob."

According to several sources, the first man assassinated by "the mob" was Willis Johnson, a former cowboy that worked for Robert DeKalb Forsythe, who came to the Brown County area in 1866 with his brother, Bud. Forsythe had been born in Polk County, Arkansas, on August 23, 1847, and came to Ellis County, Texas, with his parents at the age of four.

"In 1866, my brother, Bud, and I came to Brown County and organized the old Williams Ranch. A year or so later, we built a store and it became, in years to follow, an important trading post," Forsythe said.[1] Forsythe's recollections were published in 1931in a book by Tevis Clyde Smith.

Forsythe, then a resident of Zephyr, told writer Smith that during the time he and his brother operated the Williams ranch, he made two trail drives to New Mexico, selling the cattle at a ranch which now occupies a site of present day Roswell.

"We had 1,500 head of cattle in our first herd, and 1,800 head in the second. The best steers in those days cost us $10 per head, the best cows cost $8 per head. We doubled our money on them in New Mexico."[2]

According to Smith's story, Forsythe met a young man at the end of the first drive "who appeared to be hard put. I asked him to come over to the chuck wagon and have a hand out on me. He accepted. He said his name was Henry Ford and that he was headed for Texas. I told him that there was a wagon train in the vicinity that was bound for San Saba. He thanked me, and the next time I saw him he was on his way to San Saba with the wagoneers. He did not have a horse, but had gotten a ride on one of the wagons. Several months later, I met him in San Saba. He wanted work, and I took him back to the ranch with me and put him to punching cattle. That was a lucky day for my brother, Bud Forsythe. A few weeks later, we made our second cattle drive to the same ranch in New Mexico.[3]

According to the story, while on the New Mexico ranch Bud Forsythe and some men got into a hot poker game. One was a Mexican who had little love for gringos.

"After Bud had won several dollars from him, the Mexican shouted some words in Spanish, leaped from his chair, drew a knife and lunged at Bud. Although he was quick, he was not fast enough to elude Henry Ford who was leaning on a counter nearby. As soon as the Mexican had spoken, Ford knew what he said and what his intentions were. He yanked his pistol in a flash, shooting the Mexican as he came up with his knife. According to Forsythe's published story, the first bullet

Ford fired hit the Mexican in the shoulder, spinning him around. As the Mexican ran away to hide behind a counter, Ford went after the man, shooting him two more times.

"Things looked bad for Ford," Forsythe recalled. The Mexican had three bullet holes in his body, and was about to kick off. Then he took a turn for the better, and recovered speedily. Ford was billed for trial, but nothing ever came of it and he returned to Texas with us. We became good friends."[4]

Forsythe recalled in his interview with Smith that Ford was highly educated, could speak several languages including several Indian dialects. Before coming to Texas he had worked as an interpreter for the government dealing with tribes in Northern New Mexico territory.

Another man that worked for Forsythe at Williams Ranch was Willis Johnson, who started to buy land on his own, stocking it as he could and eventually became a well-to-do rancher.

"While apparently within the law most of the time, Johnson had many friends who were not. When his friends got into trouble Johnson always gave them a helping hand," Forsythe told Smith. "He went on the bond of more cattle rustlers than anybody who ever lived in this section of the state; he did more than just go on their bond. When the time of their trial came up, he always found good lawyers for them. As a general rule, the outlaws would succeed in beating their cases."[5]

During this time, Johnson apparently made more than his share of enemies among his neighbors for supporting the lawless element. When he helped an older man latch on to a much younger girl for a wife, it infuriated her family.

"Finally, Johnson got into a kidnapping scrape," Forsythe recalled. "He took a 16-year-old girl away from her parents and assisted her in marrying a man much older than herself. As far as the girl was concerned, she wanted to marry the man. But the parents objected to the match and took the charge to court,

27

accusing Johnson with abduction and swearing a lie in regard to the girl's age.

"Johnson's trial never came off. A few days before he was to appear in court, he was ambushed near his home. He was riding a $500 racehorse at the time, and the men who ambushed him killed both Johnson and the horse.

"Johnson's murder started the famous San Saba, McCulloch, Mills county feud, a reign of terror that lasted for a long time," Forsythe said.[6]

Forsythe guessed that over 100 people were killed during those times. The rancher said most of the men murdered during the mob days were killed in ambuscades; neither side gave the men they were after a chance to defend themselves.

The earliest mob violence was brought about as a result of a growing number of questionable people drifting into the Central Texas area to avoid military service and turning to outlawry. According to historian T. R. Havins, author of the book, *"Something About Brown, A History of Brown County, Texas,"* livestock theft was the most prevalent form of crime since the range was open and livestock often grazed miles from the home of the owner.

"Thieves encountered little difficulty in running brands or in branding unbranded, young cattle," Havins wrote. [7] Cattle rustling became more active after 1866 when John J. McCoy provided a ready market for trail herds at Abilene, Kansas.

Havins said "one notorious Brown County man was leader of a band of stock thieves that confined its depredations to the northern and western sections of the county," but he did not identify the man by name. "This leader," he said, "was indicted by the grand jury at every meeting of that body for 10 successive sessions from 1876 to 1881 on many charges of horse, cow or hog theft." None of the charges ever held true.

In April 1876, Texas Ranger Company E of the Frontier Battalion was sent to Brown County to scout out thieves and rustlers in Brown, San Saba and Lampasas counties. In a report to Austin, the ranger in command named Best reported that he had been called to Williams Ranch for the purpose of assisting in maintaining order, enforcing the law and searching for fugitives.

According to historian Havins, Best was called to Williams Ranch after a Mexican had been shot and "then swung from the limb of a tree while the murderers stood by with drawn guns and dared the citizens to attempt to remove the dead man."[8]

Like a number of other counties in the Texas Heartland, one of the worst bands of thieves was led by the notorious John Wesley Hardin.

Hardin had a number of kinsmen in the San Saba area, including his cousins the Clements, and Mannen Clements son-in-law, Jim Miller.

Ranchmen in the Williams Ranch area and along Blanket Creek suffered the worst losses. They gathered together and in March 1874 demanded Brown County Sheriff J. H. Gideon to do something about the gang. He sent a deputy named Charlie Webb to Comanche County to keep an eye on the Hardin bunch. When Hardin learned of the ranchers' demand, he boosted that he would not stop his activities and he would not submit to arrest by any sheriff or deputy. When Webb went to Williams Ranch to investigate the hanging of the Mexican with Ranger Best, he crossed trails with Hardin, Jim Taylor, Bud and Tom Dixon and Alex Barrackman. The men heckled Webb, and warned him to stay out of Comanche County.[9]

On May 26, 1874, Webb left Brown County for Comanche to visit a girlfriend. However, not long after arriving in Comanche Webb met Hardin near the northeast corner of the courthouse square. Words were passed and quickly Hardin pulled his pistol and shot Webb in the heart. According to writer Havins, Hardin and his gang fled Comanche and headed east for the brushy country along the Leon River. Ranger Captain Waller and a posse of rangers and sheriff's deputies followed in pursuit. One outlaw, Alex Barrickman, was killed, and officers captured and arrested the two Dixon boys. Taylor and Hardin escaped.[10]

Later that same day, rangers arrested John Wesley's brother, Joe Hardin, a Comanche lawyer, member of the Masonic order and a respected citizen. It is doubtful that Joe Hardin had anything to do with his brother and the gang, but he was lodged on a second floor of a building on the southeast corner of the square along with the Dixons. A new county jail was under construction nearby.

When news of Webb's death reached Brownwood, some 20 or more of Brown County's most prominent ranchers gathered near the courthouse. The men were heavily armed. Soon, additional local businessmen joined the group. Before reaching Comanche, the group had grown in number to about 40.

The Brownwood group, now a mob of grumbling men, soon disarmed the guards and took Joe Hardin and the Dixon boys to a nearby grove of live oak trees and hanged them. Joe Hardin pleaded for his life, saying he had not been involved with his brother in any law violation and had not been present when Webb was shot down. One mob member complained that Joe Hardin, a lawyer, would probably defend his brother and Taylor if they were arrested and brought to trial. That ended the conversation. Joe Hardin and the others were left dangling from a big oak limb.

According to Havins, rustlers, horse thieves, fence cutters and other lawless types continued to cause problems in Brown County for a number of years. Williams Ranch, which grew up as a frontier trading post in 1856, boosted the reputation that it was one of the most rowdy towns on the whole frontier, and on many occasions during the decade of the 1870s rangers were called on to quell the unruly element that made the community its headquarters.

[1] Tevis Clyde Smith, Frontier's Generation, A Pioneer History of Brown County, (Brownwood, TX: Greenwood Press, 1931) p. 32-34.

[2] Ibid.

[3] Ibid.

[4] Ibid.

[5] Ibid.

[6] Ibid.

[7] T. R. Havins, Something About Brown, A History of Brown County, Texas, (Brownwood, TX: Banner Printing Co., 1958) p. 26-30.

[8] Ibid.

[9] Ibid.

[10] Ibid.

Chapter 3:
See No Evil, Speak No Evil

It was known by many names, but the name "Mob" described it best regardless the area in which you were living. The late J. E. Shropshire, a pioneer lawyer who came to McCulloch County by horse-drawn wagon in mid-April 1893, experienced several dangerous episodes during those early years of frontier practice. He had graduated from the University of Texas Law School in the second such class ever held at that school in 1891.

In his unpublished memoirs, he recalled that the organization was called "The Mills County Mob," and others usually heard it referred to simply as "The Mob." However, it also was called "The Alliance."

According to tradition, the so-called mob was organized by seven wealthy ranchers for the purpose of stopping the activities of an apparent well-organized gang of cattle rustlers operating in Mills, San Saba, Brown and McCulloch counties, but was later taken over by some of the very people whose lawless operations it was created to combat.[1]

According to Shropshire's recollections, one unique feature of the Mob's operations was a fraternal-like ritual – "three degrees or obligations" – of which any law abiding citizen would have no qualms about taking. However, the third one required swearing an oath on a penalty of death for disobedience and to kill or burn out any person or persons on order of the executive committee.

Unlike many modern, secret terrorist groups, the Mob never took credit for eliminating its enemies. It was left to the general public to draw its own conclusions. As a result, the Mob perhaps was blamed for some murders that it did not commit.[2] However, the Mob did on occasion leave behind

32

signs of its involvement, including a number of bullet wounds in the victims' heads, or a note penned to the clothes of a body dangling from a tree limb.

There were lots of killings attributed to the Mob, and many instances of abuse. Texas Ranger Captain Bill McDonald, in one of his reports to superiors, noted that Mob rule in the Central Texas area had cost the lives of no less than 42 men. It was one of the bloodiest periods of outlawry in Texas history. Perhaps as many as 200 persons fled the area to seek safety for themselves and their families.

Secrecy was supreme in the organization. According to Shropshire, a man soon learned to keep his lips tightly shut, even among his own family. One man was reportedly killed because of what his child had said in school.

Early-day McCulloch County Sheriff F. M. Miller was marked for death by the Mob and his assassination was ordered. A man named Jim Longley, a friend of the sheriff, was the person appointed to do the killing. Longley refused and promptly defected from the Mob. A short time later, Longley was fired on from ambush, the bullet knocking him down and burning a crease across the back of his neck.

Shropshire recalled the following story in his unpublished memoirs:

"A young man of this town (Brady) told me of the following circumstance: He was a teen-aged lad and was hunting at night near his home. He walked upon several neighbors – men that he knew – in a gulch by a fire. They looked at him strangely, and then at one another. One said, 'shall we take him in?' The others assented.

They swore him in over a shotgun, to keep everything secret under penalty of death.

I could name the party who told me and some of the parties in the crowd, but it would do no good. Some of them are still living here and I was told the story in confidence.

So you see that was one way they had of recruiting

members. As a rule very few homesteaders entered into those nightriders and mobs. But when those things do get started they become complete outlaw organizations. They are forced into desperate measures and they sometimes involve nearly the whole community before they are suppressed," Shropshire observed.[3]

The pioneer lawyer also recalled an incident that occurred in Brown County before he moved to the Brady area. While attending the district court there, Shropshire said he heard a trial in which the confessed facts were the most disgusting he had ever heard.

"A man living out there toward the boundary of Mills County had come into the Brown County District Court, gone before the grand jury and had accused his neighbor of the most infamous crime that I had ever heard presented by an indictment. The accused man indignantly denied the charge, demanded trial and was acquitted.

The evidence showed that the prosecuting witness had maliciously perjured himself to slander his neighbor. The grand jury then returned an indictment against the falsifying witness for perjury. Imagine his defense. He admitted the perjury, but said he had to do so for fear of his life because the Mills County Mob had ordered him to do so," Shropshire said.[4]

The pioneer lawyer observed that he would never have "succumbed to such threats…those kinds of secret organizations are born of corruption, and finally are forced to live in infamy.

"That infamous Mills County Mob sent its tentacles into Brown County, thence over the river into San Saba County, and was penetrating McCulloch County when I moved here. Men were being ambushed and murdered all around until the rangers under Captain Bill McDonald moved in on it in San Saba County and dispersed the thing. Those feuds and mobs of former years had the habit, sometimes, of a prairie fire that sweeps the whole countryside," Shropshire said.[5]

34

A particularly grim murder occurred in McCulloch County on January 4, 1893, when a man named George Brown of the Voca community was taken during the night and found the next day hanging from an oak tree limb with his feet almost touching the ground. The hanging happened about four miles out of Brady on the Voca Road.

The late Wayne Spiller of Voca, who worked years compiling three volumes of McCulloch County history, said the hanging tree was about 225 yards north of Four Mile Draw on the east side of the road.

In 1966, Spiller also learned of another McCulloch County murder. A man named Bradley who lived in the north central portion of the county, was shot out of his saddle and killed in 1893. He was told later by the murdered man's son that the killer got religion a number of years later and confessed to the killing. The son planned to take revenge on his father's slayer, but his mother talked him out of it.

In the August 17, 1888 issue of the *San Saba County News,* the killing of J. Y. Criswell was announced. Criswell was shot from his wagon "and instantly killed on Thursday of last week near his home in McCulloch County. It is not known who did the shooting." [6] Records show that Criswell died on August 9, 1888, and was buried in Cowboy community cemetery.

Ironically, there may have been a witness to the Criswell shooting. In a electronic communication received on August 26, 2003, from Mozelle Gray Tonne, she relates that an uncle, Mack Gray, told a story to his nephew, Virgil Harrison, about the shooting of a man from his wagon while visiting Tonne's mother in Cross Plains in January 1980.

"He named his uncle, George Gray, and another uncle, Tom Maxwell, as being mixed up in the mob. Virgil wanted to know what it was all about and he (Uncle Mack) said the locals were upset because they felt the lawmen were not protecting them from cattle rustlers and they organized to take the law into their own hands.

"My grandfather, Mack Gray Sr., said his father sent him and his brother, William (Billy) Gray, out of the country so they would be safe from the mob.

"My grandmother, wife of Mack Sr., went out the woodpile while cooking dinner one day and heard a gunshot. She looked up just in time to see a man driving a wagon fall backward. She raised up and saw Uncle George on his horse slowly trotting across the road.

"Sometime later, when Grandma's brother and wife, John and Ellie Smith, came to visit and spend the night, Grandpa saw Uncle George outside in the dark with his gun propped on the sill of an open window holding a bead on Grandma. He yelled out for George not to shoot and put away his gun. Uncle George still held the bead and said: 'She knows too much,'" Tonne wrote.

"Uncle John said he had never before seen a grown man cry, but Grandpa was crying and begging George not to shoot. He, too, began to plead and finally George eased the gun down and left," she recalled.

According to the story, she said, things got "so hot that George and others, unnamed, went to Stonewall County and holed up in a cave on the east side of Double Mountains. A number of years later, one of Uncle John's sons, Harve, decided to go and check out the cave. Their farm was not far and he had heard the story of the hideout. Sure enough, Harve saw on the wall of the cave in his own handwriting, George W. Gray, and he even left his forwarding address: Goldthwaite, Texas."[7]

"Uncle Mack repeated to Virgil another story I had often heard of a Cade boy in the neighborhood being hanged in his own yard and even buried there because of fear to travel to a cemetery," she continued.

"Years later Uncle Mack said he once asked Uncle George if he had ever killed a man. He replied, 'I never killed one that didn't need it,'" she wrote. "George Gray lived to be a very old man and quit his old habits and Uncle Tom Maxwell became a Pentecostal preacher."[8]

Seeing too much and then talking about it could bring about a man's death warrant. In his book, *I'll Die Before I Run,* " historian C. L. Sonnichsen related a story about Squeaky Evans, one of several men who escaped being mobbed.

According to Sonnichsen, Evans lived near Cottonwood Pond about four miles north of Richland Springs. When it came his turn to be "regulated," the mob that came to kill him ran Evans through the water hole but failed to catch him. Evans left the country.

When a friend asked Evans what was wrong and why he was fleeing the county, Evans replied, "I guess I seed too much."

---

[1] Wayne Spiller, Handbook of McCulloch County History, Volume 2, (Canyon, TX: Staked Plains Press, 1986) p. 1-19.

[2] Ibid.

[3] Ibid.

[4] Ibid.

[5] Ibid.

[6] Ibid.

[7] Mozelle Gray Tonne, E-mail communication to author, August 27, 2003.

[8] Ibid.

Chapter 4:
Times Were Extra Tough

Few accounts of life in 19th Century Texas provide either the vivid personal detail or the poignancy of the recollections written by Sarah Harkey Hall in 1905. Her story, written at the age of 48 for her children, detailed the daily and seasonal life on the frontier in San Saba County.

The story chronicles her struggle for physical and emotional survival as well as the struggles of her family and community. Unlike many pioneer memoirs that were written for later generations, her story does not glide over the daily hardships of life. The story is a remarkable record that is more bitter than sweet. Just meeting the daily responsibilities of life could be difficult enough without being faced with mob violence of the most brutal kind or surprise Indian raids.

Sarah Harkey was born March 2, 1857, on Richland Creek, one mile east of Richland Springs in San Saba County. She was the fifth of 13 children who were left orphaned when her parents died in early 1869. Her father, Dan Harkey, was born in North Carolina and her mother was a native of West Virginia. They came to Texas in 1853-1854 and settled on Richland Creek, then located within the vast reaches of Bexar County. San Saba County was not then organized. The Harkey family was the first to locate in the area, once a popular campground for Comanche Indians.

The four oldest children had been taught to do the chores about the home, care for the stock and to look after the farm, but none were prepared to handle the emotional devastation that resulted from their parents' death.

Joe, the eldest, tried to keep the family together. He was unable to support his siblings by farming so he joined the Texas Rangers. His younger brother, John, left home at the age of 14 to cowboy on nearby ranches. It wasn't too long before the older girls, Jane and Julia, got married. They did welcome some of their siblings into their homes.

For Sarah, the future was grim. As the oldest child still at home, she was in charge of caring for the home, spinning yarn and making fabrics for clothing, tending the livestock and helping the younger ones to learn how to read and write and care for themselves. It was a tremendous responsibility with no adult close by to assist her or to come to the young family's aid during illnesses or if hostile Indians were raiding nearby.

"In those days everybody lived in log huts floored with puncheon or slabs, dressed on one side with a broad ax, and covered with boards made by hand," she wrote.[1]

Sarah said her parents had prospered as the years went by, having a "nice bunch of cattle, though small, and sheep, goats, hogs and a few head of horses that her father had raised from one brood mare which he kept locked in the stable every night from the Indians."

She noted in her memoirs that as the country slowly developed, there would be more conveniences for the families. A sawmill was erected on the San Saba River and there was plenty of post oak and elm timber for sawing lumber, so her father was able to build a better house.

Before mob violence engulfed the area after the Civil War, Sarah witnessed the aftermath of a Comanche Indian raid, and the picture was not pretty.

"I well remember one raid when they (Indians) killed one of our neighbors and scalped him and cut and slashed his body in the most horrible manner. Oh, such a terrible scene for innocent women and children to gaze upon; enough to almost chill the blood of anyone with a conscience. It was the first corpse my eyes ever looked upon, and it is still fresh in my mind," she recalled.[2]

Sarah was not the only author among the Harkey clan. Her younger brother, Dee Harkey, told his personal story as a

39

lawman a number of years later. His book, *Mean As Hell,* is popular among Old West collectors.

Dee Harkey was born in 1866 at Richland Springs, and was three years old when his parents died. He was raised by his sister, Sarah, and his older brother, Joe, who he later worked for as a deputy sheriff in 1882 when Joe Harkey was elected sheriff of San Saba County. The mob was busy in the region at that time.

Dee Harkey, San Saba County deputy sheriff and later New Mexico lawman and author of the book, "Mean As Hell." Photo courtesy J. Evetts Haley Collection, Haley Library, Midland.

While working with his brother, Dee Harkey tangled with Deacon Jim Miller, a cousin by marriage to outlaw John

Wesley Hardin and a killer for hire. Harkey's job as a deputy was serving warrants and arresting horse thieves and rustlers. It is believed that his dispute with Miller was over a warrant.

Notorious assassin Deacon Jim Miller, once a resident of the Texas Heartland and alleged killer of New Mexico lawman Pat Garrett. Miller was a son-in-law of Mannen Clements Sr., McCulloch and San Saba County rancher, trail driver and first cousin of John Wesley Hardin. Photo courtesy Division of Manuscripts, University of Oklahoma Libraries.

Harkey quit as deputy and married his wife, Sophie, in 1885 and moved to Bee County where he started farming. He soon got into a squabble with a neighbor, George Young, whom he killed in a knife fight in a corn patch. He moved on to New Mexico in 1890 where he went to work as a butcher in Carlsbad. A quarrel with a customer named George High resulted in two shooting incidents in which Harkey acquitted himself well.[3]

Harkey's first gunfight happened in Richland Springs in 1884. He had arrested a mule thief named Quinn, and he and another deputy named Davis had taken Quinn and his son to their hotel room to change clothes.

Suddenly, Quinn's wife and daughter, Mary, whom Harkey had been courting, burst into the room. Mary, holding a pistol, said, "Dee, that's my father and I'm going to protect him." With that, she shot Dee in the stomach.

His sidekick, Deputy Davis, ran from the room, while Harkey tackled the young woman and threw her to the floor and took the pistol away. But her father, Quinn, grabbed a brush knife and threatened to hit him with it.

Deputy Davis broke up the standoff when he led a bunch of citizens to the rescue. Harkey wanted to shoot Quinn, but was restrained. A doctor came and found that the bullet fired by the young woman had hit Harkey's watch and had only burned a blister across his belly.[4] Harkey served as a New Mexico lawman until 1911. He started ranching after retirement in Eddy County, New Mexico, and died peacefully in his 80s on June 17, 1958 in Carlsbad.

Ironically, the Harkey's had some neighbors with ranches on both sides of them that would eventually find fame but of a different sort. The Ketchum clan would see two of their sons turn outlaw, and one – Tom "Black Jack" Ketchum – would be hanged in a most gruesome way in New Mexico for attempting to rob a train.

The first of the Ketchum's came to Texas in 1846 and settled in Guadalupe County, east of San Antonio de Bexar. Another bunch came in 1848 and settled in Caldwell County, just north of Guadalupe County. Among these were Green Berry Ketchum and his young wife, Temperance, and a baby daughter, Elizabeth. Before arriving in the Texas heartland, the couple had two sons, Green Berry Jr. and Samuel Wesley. Berry was born in 1850 and Sam came along in 1854. Tom

Ketchum would come into the world in 1863.

There were few settlers in the Richland Creek area in western San Saba County when the Ketchum's chose a place to settle. The Green Berry Ketchum's appear on the 1860 census, having a personal estate valued at $4,534, and four children. The next house visited by the census taker, Assistant Marshal W. B. Coffee, was that of John L. Harkey, a farmer with the same number of children but little money. The Harkey place was sandwiched between Green Berry Ketchum and James Ketchum, also a stock raiser, who had six children, and property valued at $3,734.[5]

When the 1870 census was taken, young Tom Ketchum was just seven years old. He had already seen lots of difficulties because misfortune had started hitting the Ketchum family three years earlier. His uncle, Peter Ketchum Jr., was killed by Indians in 1866. This was the neighbor that Sarah Harkey said in her memoir that she saw dead and mutilated by the Indians.

A year later, Green Ketchum's brothers, James and John, were returning from a cattle drive to New Mexico with three other cowboys when they were ambushed near a stage coach stand on the Concho River about 60 miles west of Fort Concho. The saddlebags carried by the men were loaded with money received for the herd. When the Indians raffled through the dead men's belongings, they did not know the value of the printed notes and scattered it to the winds.

When troopers of the 4th Cavalry at Camp Charlotte were notified of the killings, they came and took the bodies of the men to a site near present day Tankersley in Tom Green County where they were buried.[6] Some of the currency was recovered and returned to the James' widow, Mary, according to a family story written by Ollie Ketchum and published in the San Saba County History book.

On October 28, 1868, Tom's father died. His older brother, Berry, 18, took over management of the ranch and also of the households. His father's death was a exceptional blow because his mother seemed to favor the older boy's management and family leadership style, leaving young Tom and his other brother, Sam, somewhat left out. Whether this caused Tom to later turn to outlawry is questionable.

Tom Ketchum's first run-in with the law came in 1876 when he and another boy, Richard "Dick" Duncan, his closest friend, were taken to court for the theft of seventy-five cents worth of property. The so-called property was believed to have been a mess of pecans taken from an orchard. When the case was called, the boys failed to show up. Another case, filed in March 1880, also was never settled.

When the 1880 census was taken, Berry and Tom Ketchum were not in San Saba County. However, the men were actively moving livestock to market during the time so that could be the reason for their absence. Both returned to San Saba County later.

Berry Ketchum left San Saba County about 1884 and moved his ranching operation to the Knickerbocker community in Tom Green County, about 100 miles west of the San Saba area. He was a successful cattleman, and needed room for his growing herd. Some of his family, including Sam and Tom, followed along in subsequent years, along with some members of the Duncan family and others seeking more open range.

Ketchum was a hard-drinking cowboy who exhibited strange behavior from time to time. For example, when his attentions to a young woman were rejected, he commenced to beat himself about the head and body with his lariat and pistol. While in New Mexico, Ketchum started robbing stagecoaches, banks and trains. His brother, Sam, helped him on some of these forays. During one train robbery, Sam was seriously wounded and later died.

On August 16, 1899, Tom Ketchum attempted to rob single-handed a Colorado and Southern Railroad train near Folsum, Arizona. During the robbery, Ketchum shot the express messenger in the jaw before exchanging shots with the conductor, Frank Harrington. Harrington was struck in the neck and Tom's right arm was shattered by a load of buckshot. Ketchum dropped his pistol, crawled beneath the train and into the brush. He was found the next day by a freight train crew propped against a tree near the tracks. Doctors had to amputate his mutilated arm.[7]

Tom Ketchum was hanged outside the County Jail at Clayton, New Mexico, on April 26, 1901. Due to a miscalculation about the drop, Ketchum's head was severed from his body by the fall. It was a very gruesome scene, and photographs of the event are an Old West collector's item.

Sarah Harkey continued to look after her siblings until she was 20 years old. She had met Dave Hall at a neighborhood gathering. He was uneducated but a hard worker and from a good family. Hall was descended from John Mabin Hall, who was another early day settler in the area.

Sarah and Dave Hall were married in October 1875. She had not told her brother, Joe, in advance of the wedding, and he was not pleased with her choice of a husband. However, all the Harkey siblings found a haven with Sarah even after her marriage to Hall.

According to Sarah's memoirs, Dave Hall was a good man but he had strange ways. He was difficult to communicate with, and he was demanding of his wife. Even when she was sickly, she said, he asked her to go and stay with his sister who did not need any assistance.

As their family grew, he would leave the home place for several days at a time and return home broke and with a hangover. Despite these failures as a husband, Dave Hall was a good father and tended to his young brood when his wife was sick or during a pregnancy.

"Dave's ways worried me no little, and kept me in deep wonder. I couldn't understand him and had always said I if I ever got married I never would quarrel with my husband,"

Sarah Hall wrote.[8]

---

[1] Sarah Harkey Hall, Surviving on the Texas Frontier, The journal of An Orphan Girl in San Saba County, (Austin, TX: Eakin Press, 1996) p. 5.

[2] Ibid., p. 6.

[3] Bill O'Neal, Encyclopedia of Western Gunfighters, (Norman, OK: University of Oklahoma Press, Norman, 1979) p. 131.

[4] Ibid., p. 131.

[5] Jeffrey Burton, The Deadliest Outlaws, (England: A Palomino Book, 2007) p. 15.

[6] Ibid., p. 16.

[7] O'Neal, op. cit., p. 176.

[8] Hall, op. cit., p. 74.

Chapter 5:
"Summer Names," Or Aliases

The Central Texas mobs were gradually ridding the territory of outlaws, horse thieves, rustlers, fence-cutters and other unsavory characters during the years following the Civil War.

Among those being encouraged to leave were a couple of toughs from the area named Dave Kemp and Daniel Bogan of Hamilton County, alias Bill Gatlin, Bill McCoy and perhaps other names chosen to avoid arrest. A lot of the cowboys working the range in those days had gotten into trouble and would use assumed names to avoid the law. The cowboys called the practice taking "summer names."

The man named Gatlin got into some serious trouble after leaving Hamilton County in the Texas heartland. Like others, Gatlin traveled to Tascosa in the Texas Panhandle where he got involved with a rustler gang. He had been stealing livestock so he knew the ropes.

The LS Ranch, one of the larger cattle operations on the High Plains, was losing too many cattle to rustlers. Its owner, W.M.D. Lee, called "Alphabet" because of his initials, brought in the noted New Mexico territory lawman, Pat Garrett, to put an end to the stealing.

Garrett was offered $5,000 a year if he would lead the "Home Rangers,"[1] a group of LS cowboys selected to hunt down thieves. These so-called rangers were not Texas Rangers, but the force got the blessing of then Texas Governor John Ireland.

Garrett, who had made a name for himself as Lincoln County sheriff by killing Billy the Kid, got another incentive to take the job; a man named Jordan McAllister, working for Lee, told the New Mexico lawman if he took the job, he would sell him some prize cattle at a quarter of their market value with a promise to buy them back at full price when the area was cleaned up of rustlers.[2]

Garrett started to work in the spring of 1884. He tried to do the job as legal as possible, asking the governor for a fugitive list, getting his cowboy rangers commissions and telling the big ranch companies that he could not do anything without (legal) papers.[3]

When roundup work began, Garrett and his "home rangers" were checking the range camps looking for fugitives and others suspected of cattle theft and other offenses. Gatlin was among a bunch of suspected rustlers who were surrounded in their shack on a cold February day in 1885. When Garrett called out for the men to surrender, nine came out of the cabin, but Gatlin and another man, Charley Thompson, refused.

After some discussion, Thompson agreed to come out but Gatlin continued to stay holed up. The standoff lasted most of the day until Garrett got disgusted. He had two men get on top of the cabin and yank off the roof poles. Gatlin challenged Garrett and others to come in and take him. They did before a shot was fired. Gatlin was taken to Tuscosa and jailed, but a careless guard allowed him to escape.

Daniel Bogan, alias Bill Gatlin alias Bill McCoy had made a bad reputation for himself before leaving Central Texas. According to one historian, Gatlin was one of a breed of men ranging through central and western Texas who would "Kill a man to check whether the gun was loaded." Bogan was on the governor's fugitive list, wanted as an accessory to murder in Hamilton County.

After the Civil War, two gangs – the Blue Ridge Bunch and the River Bunch – were in competition for control of the county. Bogan, aka Gatlin, was suspected of being involved in the 1880 murder of a local cattleman named William Snell. Also involved was David Kemp. The Bogan boys and Kemp were close friends, spending a lot of their time in Hamilton drinking emporiums.

Kemp was more than just a friend to Dan and Bill Bogan. He was their brother-in-law, having been married to one of the Bogan sisters in 1881. However, the marriage did not last after he went to the state penitentiary in 1883 for killing local rancher Daniel "Doll" Smith during a senseless dispute over Smith's wagon being blocked by Kemp and Bogan horses outside a meat market on the Hamilton town square. Kemp did not stay long in Huntsville. He was given a conditional pardon by Governor John Ireland on January 17, 1887, reportedly because of his youth.

Kemp was born on March 1, 1862, in Hamilton County, and by the time he was a teenager, he had been involved in several violent episodes in his home territory.

Kemp's travels were unusual for those times. Most farm boys never got more than 25 miles from their homes, but he and Bogan traveled about 600 miles by horseback to Tascosa from the Central Texas area.

During a career draped in violence, Kemp went from being a convicted killer condemned to hang in Texas to be elected county sheriff in New Mexico territory.

As a result of losing a political race to another noted shootist, some deep animosity developed between the men. In a fracas at Carlsbad, New Mexico, on February 18, 1897, Kemp and an accomplice, Will Kennon, ambushed Sheriff Les Dow outside of the Carlsbad Post Office. [4] Kemp shot Dow in the face while he was reading a letter. Although Dow drew his gun, he collapsed and died the next morning. Kemp was acquitted of the murder charge when he pleaded self-defense.

Despite his violent life style, Kemp lived to be 73 years old. Dee Harkey, another Central Texas born lawman, wrote in his memoirs that Kemp had been shot to death at his ranch near Higgins, Texas, by his sister. However, western writer-historian Robert K. DeArment notes that Harkey's report is based on an unfounded rumor that spread about in Eddy and

Chaves counties in New Mexico. DeArment says Kemp died of a massive heart attack at his ranch on January 4, 1935.

Bogan, alias Gatlin, had taken flight from Tascosa after getting into trouble over shooting a saloonkeeper. He traveled to Wyoming using the name of William McCoy, and worked as a cowboy and also on a railroad construction gang. In 1886, Bogan, alias McCoy reportedly killed a constable named Charlie Gunn. McCoy and Gunn had bad blood between them, thus the shooting scrape.

A lawman friend of Gunn, a deputy sheriff named Johnny Owens, finally took McCoy into custody after a shootout in which Bogan, alias McCoy was wounded. He was quickly bound over to the Cheyenne, Wyoming district court and held without bond. Owens put Bogan in shackles and held him in the back room of a saloon in Lusk since the frontier town did not have a jail. The deputy was afraid that a local mob might take the man and hang him, so he also put him under guard, but learned later that the guards were among Bogan's friends. He escaped during the night into a snowstorm.

Owens knew that Bogan could not travel far in the snowstorm, or with the wounds he suffered. He figured the outlaw was hiding out nearby in a ranch line camp. His assumption was correct. About two weeks after the escape, Bogan sent word that he needed medical attention. His wounds were festered and he was burning with fever. When he recovered sufficiently from his wounds, Bogan was taken to the Laramie County Jail for safekeeping.

Bogan, alias McCoy, became instantly newsworthy and relished the celebrity. A friendly sort, when not drinking, Bogan had lots of friends in that area. Soon, several members of the powerful Wyoming Stock Growers Association offered to help him and arranged for a strong defense team of lawyers to get him get out of jail and the courthouse.

After several trial delays and a change of judges, Bogan was tried for murder in August 1887. Surprisingly, Hamilton

County Sheriff J. W. Massie traveled from Texas to Wyoming for the trial. If Bogan was found not guilty of the Wyoming murder charge, Massie had a Texas arrest warrant claiming Bogan to be fugitive from justice.

On September 7, 1887, after 19 hours of deliberations, a jury found Bogan guilty of murder. The conviction carried an automatic death sentence so Bogan heard the judge, Samuel Corn, pronounce that he be hanged by the neck until he was "dead, dead, dead."[5]

Despite the seriousness of the sentence, Bogan is said to have been "completely unconcerned." He still had some friends who could help him.

A Wyoming rancher friend who was known as Tom Hall, also was on the Texas fugitive list. Hall, believed to be Tom Nichols, had known Bogan at Tascosa in the Texas Panhandle. He helped Bogan escape from jail by hiring a professional safe cracker named James Jones to commit a minor crime, get locked up in the jail with Bogan and help him saw his way out using smuggled saw blades.

On October 4, 1887, Bogan, Jones and two accused horse thieves, Charles LeRoy and William Steary, broke out. Tom Hall was waiting outside with a horse for Bogan. The two men quickly rode out of Cheyenne, kicking off one of the biggest manhunts in Wyoming history.[6] A $1,000 reward was posted for Bogan, dead or alive.

Despite the big reward being offered, Bogan, alias McCoy, alias Bill Gatlin, disappeared. Some say he went to South America; others say he hid out in the desert Southwest, perhaps Mexico, married, raised a family and became a successful rancher. He was even reported killed by a Mexican in a gunfight near El Paso, and a newspaper story in 1907 stated he had been thrown off a horse and died from a broken neck.

In 1931, a Wyoming newspaper reported that a Bogan acquaintance, A. C. Campbell, told them the last time he heard of Bogan "he had married, owned a ranch somewhere in Texas, and was branding mavericks and raising Hoover Democrats."[7]

[1] Frederick Nolan, Tascosa, Its Life and Gaudy Times, (Lubbock, TX: Texas Tech University Press, 2007) p. 165.

[2] Ibid., Page 165.

[3] Ibid., Page 167.

[4] Bill O'Neal, Encyclopedia of Western Gunfighters, (Norman, OK: University of Oklahoma Press, 1979) p. 175.

[5] Robert K. DeArment, Deadly Dozen, Twelve Forgotten Gunfighters of the Old West, (Norman, OK: University of Oklahoma Press, 2003) p. 165.

[6] Ibid., Page 165.

[7] Ibid., Page 168.

Chapter 6:
Leave Or Die

"Dutchman, get out of San Saba County."

Those words rang loud as the rope tightened about Joseph Vogel's throat. The mob had paid him and his wife, Belle, a visit to their farm in northwest San Saba County and set about hanging the man, pulling him up off the ground to let him swing and choke.

Eventually, they dropped him and gave him the order to leave. Vogel and his wife quickly moved to neighboring McCulloch County where their son, Luke, was born in 1902.

This story was told to Luke Vogel by his father while he was growing up in the Lohn area in northwest McCulloch County. Luke Vogel, who died in Brady on March 18, 1999 at the age of 96, later would be elected sheriff of McCulloch County and serve in that position for 22 years. He passed the story of his father's narrow escape from the mob to retired Texas Ranger Lt. Bob Favor when the ranger was serving in McCulloch County.

"Luther Neal was a Texas Ranger that came to San Saba County with other rangers to put the mob out of business," Favor said. "Mr. Vogel held Luther Neal in high esteem so he named his son, Luke Neal Vogel."[1]

According to a family member, W. T. Vogel, the mob had come to silence Joseph Vogel who had seen a bunch of men leave the so-called "Buzzard's Waterhole" located nearby the Vogel farm. Several calves had been stolen from the Vogel place and remains of butchered calves were found at the waterhole where the men had met the night before. A number of sticks were scattered about the area which had been used to broil meat.[2]

There were many instances of men and their families

being run out of San Saba and other nearby counties. It was a matter of leaving or facing the threat of death or injury or perhaps economic ruin.

Many early settlers left their homes when mob violence became more than they could handle, thus homes like this soon deteriorated. Photo by Bob Zeller, San Angelo.

In the mid-1930s, Mrs. Robert Lindsey, then 59 years old, recalled going to her grandfather's place in San Saba County when she was about 12 years old. While living with her grandfather, a mob of ranchers sought to control the county and force other ranchers to leave. She was interviewed by Woody Phipps of Fort Worth, one of the many unemployed Texas writers taking part in the government sponsored Federal Writers' Project that was conducted between 1936 and 1940. The interviews became a part of the American Life Histories series that can now be found on the internet.

"They (my grandparents) operated a small ranch, but it was one of the best grassed and watered places around that part of the country," she said. "That made it valuable and several ranchers were always deviling grandfather to sell out, He wouldn't do it because that was his home, and if he sold it he would not have a place to live."

Mrs. Lindsey recalled that the mob "sent my grandfather notice after notice, but he would not bluff. I saw several of the notices, and they would have a crude scaffold drawn on them. They killed old Hartman's son over some little something or other and buried him in the sand. The Hartmans lived about three-fourths of a mile from us and we would go down there real often to see how they were getting along. If we went at night, they would never have a light because they were afraid some of the gang would sneak up and shoot one of them through the window."[3]

Texas Ranger W.J.L. Sullivan, one of the first lawmen ordered to go into San Saba County to stop violence, recalled the Hartman murder in his memoirs. A man came to the hotel where Sullivan and the other rangers were staying and asked to speak with them.

"When we got downstairs we met Nat Hartman whose home was on the Colorado River. He seemed very anxious about something and informed us that his brother, Edd Hartman, was missing and that he feared that he had been killed. The Hartmans were members of the anti-mob faction, and Nat Hartman told us that this was the first time in nine years that his brother had been outside his house after sundown," Sullivan related.[4]

Sullivan told Hartman that he would need to have the county sheriff, a man named Howard or Hawkins, to accompany the rangers in the search for his brother. Nat Hartman was reluctant to ask the sheriff because people said he was a member of the mob, but he did as instructed.

Sullivan and the other lawmen arrived at Hartman's farm

a little after daylight and started the search. After walking about three-quarters of a mile, "we found the dead body of the man for whom we are searching," Sullivan wrote. Foot tracks belonging to two men also were found near the body and led to a nearby house, occupied by the John Campbell family.

In notes collected in the early 1980s, writer Nedrah Stringfellow Magnan of Burnet and formerly of Richland Springs and San Saba, conducted interviews with several persons, including Mrs. M. S. Hagen, widow of W. J. "Billie" Brice, Mrs. Calvin Raney, Charles Schneider and others about mob violence. She had a newswoman's curiosity about those early events as her father, Ned Stringfellow, had been the longtime editor and publisher of the *Richland Springs Eye-Witness,* an early-day weekly newspaper.

In one interview, she learned that Edd Hartman rented land owned by Dick Murray on the Colorado River, neighboring John Campbell. Hartman had a fine patch of corn growing close to the Campbell property. A fence kept Campbell's hogs from getting in Hartman's cornfield. However, the fence had fallen down and Hartman had to drive the hogs out. He called on Campbell three times concerning the hogs and even offered to help build a pen and feed the hogs until he could gather his crop.

As Hartman was driving the hogs from the field though a gap in the fence, Campbell was laying in wait for him under a big tree. Campbell's sons, Mick and Jim, were with him and he was going to make them kill Hartman while he held him.

"Don't get my boys into any trouble," the mother cried out. The youngsters ran into the house.

While holding Hartman down, Campbell stabbed him to death, then scattered corn kernels on the ground so the hogs would destroy any bloodstains or other evidence of the struggle. Campbell's wife, angry that he would try and involve his children in the affair, told him she would testify against him in court. "You better not," Campbell declared before leaving the place.

The dead man's body was taken to brother Nat Hartman's place where an inquest was held concerning the murder.

According to the story told by Mrs. Raney to Magnan, a few days later a neighbor of the Campbells, a Mrs. Murray, went for a visit to see how Mrs. Campbell and the boys were doing. While there, she asked for a drink of cool water. Mrs. Campbell took a bucket and walked down to the river to fetch some fresh water, but she did not return. A search for the woman was conducted but there was no trace of her to be found.

"Several days later a foot was seen protruding from the river waters. A weight had been tied to the body but it was not strong enough to hold the body down. A bucket was found nearby on a sandbar along with a man's footprint. The body was that of Mrs. Campbell," writes Magnan.

Campbell was indicted for murder in the stabbing of Edd Hartman by a San Saba Grand Jury, but his trial was moved to Fort Mason on a change of venue. He was convicted of Hartman's murder and given a sentence of seven and a half years in the state penitentiary but he appealed the case.

"He was tried sixteen times in eight years, and finally got off on a light sentence of two and half years, and went to the penitentiary from Lampasas to serve it out. I had to go to court twice a year for eight years to testify in that case," Sullivan recalled.[5] No one was charged in the drowning death of Campbell's wife.

Other people have related stories about members of their families having to vacate the area due to mob violence.

Judith M. Nickles of Fort Worth and San Angelo notes that according to a family story, her paternal great-grandfather (unnamed) rode with the Vigilantes in San Saba – to a point. "The story goes, as I remember it, that he would be gone for days and, upon returning home, his wife would ask, "Did you find the man you were looking for?"

"Yes," he would reply.

"What did you do with him?"

"Hung him."

The end came when there was a further division in the group, she said. This time, he refused to take sides.

"A group of men paid him a friendly visit to say that if he did not make a choice they would not be responsible for his safety or that of his family. He told them that if they would give him a little time he would sell out and leave the county."

Around 1890 he moved his family to Greer County, Oklahoma, she said.

"It was not the first time that my great-grandfather had pulled up stakes because of violence. In 1876 he shot and killed his stepfather and fled from northeast Arkansas to Hood County, Texas. The story goes that the law caught up with him, told him that the man needed killing, and said to come on back home. Whether he ever went back home or not, I cannot determine, but I do know that the grand jury found a no bill scarcely two weeks later.

"On the other side of my family, my maternal grandfather, born in 1873, moved to Lampasas where he was about five and was well acquainted with the feuds there – notably the Higgins-Horrell bunch. He went to school with at least one of the Horrells. I literally grew up at Grandpa's knee listening to his tales and ended up with a master's degree in history because of the fascination that he sparked in me," she said.[6]

In 1967, Henry C. Short of Fayetteville, Arkansas, wrote a letter to Mrs. James Seals of Cedar Park, in Williamson County, and near Austin. He told her that his parents, George W. Short and Mary Matilda Nash Short, were originally from Navarro County, Texas, and both are buried in the Rochelle Cemetery in McCulloch County. According to Henry Short, his father, George W., was a cowboy and moved around a lot, living first in Wise County, and later worked on ranches in

McCulloch, Tarrant, San Saba, Coryell, Mills, Brazos, Bastrop and Bell counties. He had a brother, James, who lived west of Fort Worth, and two others who lived in Indian Territory, later the state of Oklahoma.

Henry C. Short remembered his mother telling him that the family left McCulloch County twice because "there was so much mobbing." One night when his father was nearly home, two masked men stopped him, but one said he was not the one they were looking for and they let him ride on home, warning him to stay inside the house after his arrival. Mr. Short moved his family to a safer place for fear that the outlaws would suspect that he had recognized them – "at that time it paid to keep your mouth shut," Short wrote.[7]

Riley Harkey, who lived at Harkeyville just west of San Saba, traveled to East Texas to hire two Negro families to come to San Saba to help pick his cotton, but men with masks approached him and told him to get rid of the blacks. Harkey told the masked men that he had to have them to harvest his crop as he could not get hire local laborers. The mobsters gave Harkey 24 hours to get rid of the black families or they would get rid of him.

The next afternoon they returned. Harkey's son, Jack, went out to meet them at the yard fence. One of the men got off his horse and removed a long quirt with the intention of using it to whip Jack. His father, Riley, was seated at a window with his gun. He yelled out that they had come far enough, and that he was prepared to protect himself, his family and his possessions. The man remounted and the mobsters rode away. What Riley did not know was the Negroes had also been visited by the masked riders and had been told "to leave or else" and had left the Harkey place that morning. Riley Harkey never had any more trouble from the mob.[8]

Another story collected by Mrs. Magnan related an incident that happened during a brush arbor church service.

Aunt Lit Davidson, wife of Kelly Davidson, attended a

brush arbor service with her young children. It was the custom of the times for a man's hat to be placed near the alter and people would pass by and drop an offering in it. Four horsemen arrived at the arbor, unmasked, walked to the front and dropped in their contributions.

Aunt Lit gathered up her children and spoke out to the effect – calling the men's names – saying they were guilty of killing and terrifying innocent people and if the church welcomed such people within their midst she was leaving. She did leave and never returned. "It was a brave act to name these men in public," Magnan said.[9]

Another person ordered to leave the territory got a letter of warning from the mob. The letter, sent to J. D. Montgomery, was later printed in the Richland Springs newspaper. It stated:

> Mr. Gim Mungumry, This will give you warning to get out of the country and all your folks before court time and not be at the grand jury. You turn Favers off tonight now and tell him you don't want to prosecute nobody. You talk too much. Take warning as we will come to see you. Mob Law.
>
> On the back of the letter was the outline of a coffin and the word "cofin" printed in blood. The signature "Mob Law" also was written in blood.
>
> Mr. Montgomery brought the letter to the sheriff and turned it over to him for safekeeping.
>
> Mr. Montgomery is the father of the little girl upon whom V. E. Bourland, who is now in jail, is charged with having made an assault with intent to rape.
>
> To leave the country before the grand jury meets on any kind of notice doesn't go anymore in this county and the officers will see that every witness shall have full protection. Justice will not be thwarted by any blood written notices. The criminal and coward who wrote this notice will likely have business before the

grand jury. The assistance of all law abiding and law loving people will be given to protect Mr. Montgomery and to bring the sneaking writer of the notice to the punishment he deserves.[10]

This notice was published in 1905, so mob violence continued to rare its ugly head long after the turn of the century.

[1] Bob Favor, E-mail communication to author, July 6, 2005.

[2] San Saba County Historical Commission, San Saba County History, 1856-1983, (San Saba, TX: San Saba County Historical Commission, 1983) p. 332.

[3] American Life Histories: Manuscripts from the Federal Writers' Project, 1936-1940, <http://lcweb2.loc.gov/wpaintro/wpahome.html>

[4] W. J. L. Sullivan, Twelve Years in the Saddle with the Texas Rangers, (Lincoln, NE: University of Nebraska Press, 2001) p. 39.

[5] Ibid., p. 40.

[6] Judith M. Nickles, E-mail communication to author, July 28, 2003.

[7] "A Short Reminiscence," Austin Genealogical Society Quarterly, Volume XXII, No. 3: p. 144.

[8] Mob notes from the Nedrah Stringfellow Magnan collection.

[9] Ibid.

[10] "Warned to Leave," Richland Springs Eye-Witness, Sept. 7, 1905.

Chapter 7:
Curiosity Kills

Tom Ellis was like many young schoolteachers on the frontier. He was curious about activities going on around him. Tragically, Ellis would forfeit his life for the opportunity to ride with mobsters when a band of them went across the Colorado River into Brown County for the purpose of ridding the area of a man who was accused of being involved with a gang of thieves. Young Ellis should have known better to get involved in something so sinister. His older brother, John, was a Methodist preacher and both were considered upstanding members of the community.[1]

Ellis was allowed to go along with the masked riders, but out of curiosity he violated orders and slipped up on the house where the victim was believed to be hiding. However, something scared the young teacher. Perhaps it was a rabbit or armadillo scurrying away through the high weeds. He jumped up and ran for the brush where his friends were hiding. When the men saw a figure dashing for the brush, they immediately thought it was the man they were seeking. Ellis was quickly shot down, a bullet in his heart. Many say he was one of the first victims of the newly organized mob.

Ellis' body was thrown over the back of a horse and taken to the house of Jap Snelling, who lived in the Locker community. No one accused Snelling of the killing because the body showed signs of being thrown over a saddle and carried for a considerable distance.

Sometime later, two men who had taken part in the nighttime ambush in which Ellis was killed got drunk in a Lampasas saloon, and they laughed about how the horse had pitched when they laid Ellis' body across the saddle. Within days, both were shot dead by unknown assassins, showing that a mob member had to keep his mouth shut if he hoped to stay alive.[2]

This nocturnal creature, covered in its armored skin, may have been the reason the young schoolteacher became frightened, thus leading to his accidental slaying. Photo by Bob Zeller, San Angelo.

The late Charles Leland Sonnichsen, noted historian and teacher, attempted to tell the story of the Central Texas mobs and other feuds that gripped Texas during a very bloody period following the Civil War. He gathered enough material to fill one chapter in his book, *I'll Die Before I Run,* published in 1951 by Harper and Brothers of New York. His research in Central Texas was particularly difficult because the mobs were secret organizations that kept no records of meetings, activities or lists of membership. The penalty for "talking" was death, whether the person talking belonged to the group or not. [3] The veteran writer found out quickly that it was almost impossible to find out about the past because residents would not discuss those terrible, violent days with strangers. Much of what is told about the mobs today is folklore. However, enough information has been passed down from generation to generation to provide a fairly clear picture of that bloody time.

No one can say for sure when the mob violence started to get out of hand. The late Archie Douglas Hanna says it commenced in 1886. Hanna, in his unpublished memoirs, says he was raised on the Colorado River in what is now Brown County. The area was first settled by his grandfather, Jesse P. Hanna, in 1856, two years before Brown County was officially organized.[4]

One hundred twenty-five years ago, there was of record a number of mobs operating in the Texas Heartland, specifically in San Saba, Llano, Lampasas, Mills, Coryell, Hamilton, Brown, Burnet and McCulloch counties. Following the Civil War, the entire region was on the fringe of the Texas frontier. Cattle rustlers, horse thieves and other unsavory characters moved about freely, sometimes aided by friends or confederates who posed as respectable farmers and ranchers. The mobs, or vigilante groups, were organized to combat this situation and to run undesirables out of the country or hang them if they would not leave.[5]

Vigilante Justice is not new to America. According to researchers, vigilantism arose in the Deep South and the Old West in the 1700s and 1800s when, in the absence of law enforcement officers and adequate courts, various groups, or vigilante committees, got together to blacklist, harass, banish, "tar and feather," flog, mutilate, torture, hang or shoot people who were perceived to be threats to their communities, families, privileges or economic futures. These groups have been called a number of names; lynch mobs, regulators, the alliance, raiders, masked raiders and hoo-doos.

The state of Montana perhaps holds the record for the bloodiest mob movement when a hundred or more suspected horse thieves and cattle rustlers were rounded up and killed from 1863 to 1865. Texas probably holds second place, followed by California and Dixieland states.[6]

Hanna remembers as a teenager while living in the Cottonwood Pond community about four miles north of Richland Springs and tending cattle for his father that he would see groups of men gathered in the woods and see "things going on that looked very strange to me. Sometimes twenty or thirty men riding in pairs would pass going in the same direction. In a day or two I'd hear it talked that a man had been found killed, shot to death or hanging to a tree."[7]

Another time, Hanna and his younger brother rode horseback down the river about fifteen miles and found four head of cattle that had drifted away from the home range. There were no fences in those days. The boys drove the cattle home through the woods to Cottonwood Pond.

"When we made it to the house, our folks told us that they had found Mr. Cowan had been killed that day, shot to death as he was riding the range about two miles east of the pond. We had driven the cattle through that part of the woods though we had not seen or heard any disturbance."[8]

Hanna says that at the time his family was living at Cottonwood Pond, his grandparents, George and Parthena Vest, had charge of the settlement. George Vest was a Methodist preacher, as well as one of his four sons, Asberry Vest. The other boys were Pate, Jasper and Harve. His daughter, Bettie, had married a young man named Aaron Meek.

"Anywhere among these people that I wanted to stop and stay, I was at home," Hanna noted.

Hanna remembered that one day a man came riding up to his Uncle Asberry's place at a full gallop. When the man got his breath after an apparent long ride, he asked Asberry if he had a wagon with bows and sheets. The man said he needed the wagon so he could "put Scrappy and the little ones in some bedding and food and leave this country." He then told Asberry that the men who had killed Willis Johnson would kill him and not be long about it. He offered to pay for the rig, bows and wagon sheeting with some of his cattle. "You go out on the range and any livestock, horses or cattle you see branded SEX, take them, few or many. I can't take them with me," the man declared. Hanna said that the man, Jim Sexton, and his family were never seen in that part of Texas again.

Hanna's Uncle Harvey was working on the construction of a stock-watering tank on some land that he had started using along the foot of a long mountain. He was suddenly surrounded by a bunch of men, and told to drop his tools and come out onto the bank. "We have some business with you," one said.

As soon as Harvey Vest stepped out of the excavation, men grabbed each arm and held them while another man came up with a butcher knife that he used to circle his throat.

"Harve, have your old deer piece with you and if you see Jim Sexton bring him down and you and yours will be all right from now on." Hanna said his Uncle Harvey knew nearly all the men and had long acquaintance with some of them. What the man meant by "the old deer piece" was a long rifle that Harvey Vest kept to shoot deer with. That was the mob's way of initiating one that they wanted in with them. It did not work with Harve.[9]

Sonnichsen says many early episodes dealing with the mobs in Central Texas come about through oral tradition. However, by 1888 conditions were getting so bad that various newspaper editors were taking notice and starting to write stories about the violence. *The San Saba News,* one of the oldest newspapers in the state, reported in its April 17, 1888, issue that "C. W. Smith, who lives some 12 or 15 miles north of town, was shot Tuesday evening late, near his home. There were 10 shots fired at him, but only one struck him. That has been extracted and no serious results are anticipated. It is supposed that this is another result of the feud which has existed in that section for several months, and which has already resulted in the loss of several citizens to this county, Brown, McCulloch and Mills County."[10]

Many in the San Saba area are of the opinion that the Mob got Smith on the second try. He disappeared a short time later after he was shot. One story reports that Smith's rifle was discovered in a cave along the Colorado River and everyone supposed that his body had been hidden in the cave and later washed away by high water.

Laura E. Ethridge, who was born and raised near Mullin in Mills County, is a granddaughter of Charley Smith.

"My mother was from San Saba County. Her father was killed by the Mob and his body was never found. He left home that morning with his son-in-law, both on horseback. They apparently separated and went different ways. My grandfather, Charles Smith, never came home but his horse did with his rifle still in the scabbard with bloody handprints. My cousin's family still has that gun. My father was 21 years old when that happened, and in fact he helped hunt for my grandfather's body. He said they looked everywhere, in caves, in streams and ponds, but never found a trace. It was thought that the son-in-law probably set him up for an ambush.

"My mother was very reluctant to talk of those times because they were so tragic and painful. It was the thought that the reason my grandfather was killed was that he knew many of the members of the mob. He had been asked to join them and would not, so he had to be eliminated."[11]

Archie "Doug" Hanna recalled Smith's disappearance and the search for the man.

"Uncle Dave Williams, an early settler of San Saba County, owned a good farm that covered a valley on the south side of the Colorado River and joined down against the mouth of Cottonwood Creek. He and his sons – Frank, George and Wallace – with their families lived on and cultivated the farm and tended to their livestock that ranged in the country.

"One day Frank was plowing in the field on the east side next to the mouth of the creek. He heard a man hollering that was in awful distress. He stopped plowing and listened, and in

67

a little bit he could hear nothing more of the disturbance. The next day it was reported that Charley Smith was missing. His horse with saddle on had returned home. Charley was a family man – with wife and several children. Charley's wife and children were begging that his body be found and be given a Christian burial," Hanna wrote.[12]

According to Hanna's memoirs, Williams joined the crowd that was riding and apparently hunting for the body. He mentioned to a neighbor also participating in the search that if they would search the deep hole of water in the river at the mouth of the creek that they would find Smith's body.

"Frank, you just keep quiet," the neighbor replied. "We don't want to find the body." The search went on.[13]

"It is plain to see that the mob caught Charley Smith and murdered him in the same manner other than by shooting. There was no shooting or Frank Williams would have heard it. A man told me that he believed they hung him until he was dead, then tied rocks to the body and sank it in that deep hole of water. He was never found," Hanna wrote. "No use thinking otherwise as there were some men in the searching parties that were members of the mob and some that were not."[14]

Hanna called the mob members "bloodthirsty white-livered hyenas" that thought they could not afford for any human people to ever see any more of their cruelty. He observed, "that the Indians when they used to come were not cruel at all compared to the mob." He surmised that the reason Smith's body was hidden because his body was so mutilated the mob did not want it to be found.

While the search was going on, a man named Ace Brown was found hanging in a tree. Hanna recalled that a man who was working with the search party told him that Jim Brown, Ace's son, was the first person to see his father hanging. Jim Brown was riding alone when he discovered his father's body. He fired his gun as a signal and others came to the scene.

When Ace Brown was found, it was plain that it was the

work of the mob, but he had not been shot nine times as was the custom at a mob assassination. Hanna believes that those of the mob that hanged Brown knew that shots would bring some of the searchers to the area, so he was hanged quickly and the mob members fled.

"Ace was a hunchback but when he was found hanging there was no hump in his back and his feet sat flat on the ground. Those that had hanged him had not pulled him so high that when the hump straightened out, his feet set flat on the ground," Hanna wrote. [15]

Historian Sonnichsen says that for whatever reason, Brown was not afforded the usual custom of assassination but was lynched instead. The killing caused some unexpected consequences. A respectable rancher named Leroy G. Beck happened along just as the mob finished its nasty work stringing up Brown. According to mob ethics there was nothing to do but take him into custody, try him, and sentence him to hang, all which was done in just a few minutes. Beck was good at pleading his case for survival, and promised that if the mob let him go he would sell his livestock, dispose of his ranch and be out of the country in four days.

The mob accepted his plea, and let him go. On the afternoon of the fourth day, however, two men rode up to him as he drove his wagon and team down the road near his house in Mills County and shot him to death. Beck's young granddaughter was riding in the wagon with him, but was not harmed. She told neighbors later she believed the gunmen were Negroes. This led folks to believe the men wore black masks. [16] No one was ever arrested and charged with Beck's murder.

As the violence increased, there was many voicing opposition and concern over the killings and lynching. By 1888, it was difficult to determine whose side some of the people were on. Undoubtedly, some mob members were slain but were never identified as mobsters.

While some were murdered if they failed to do as the

mob ordered, many others were able to get out of the territory and live. Among them were Squeaky Evans, who escaped the regulators at his place near Cottonwood Pond, and Joe Murphy, who was run off his place by a bunch of fifteen to twenty men shooting at him at every jump.

Evans escaped by running helter-skelter through the water hole. He later told a friend that the mob was after him because "I guess I seed (sic) too much." Murphy became a deputy sheriff in Stephens County and would later give damning testimony when some of the mob cases came into court.[17]

Hanna recalls that Uncle Dave Williams rode out one day to look for a cow and her young calf. As he rode through a brush thicket, he found a bunch of saddled horses tied to brush and a group of men busy squatting down and talking among themselves. They arose to their feet as he approached them on horseback.

One of the men called out: "Get down Mr. Williams." Uncle Dave declined, saying he needed to find his cow and calf. Three men got to their feet and approached him, calling him "Brother Williams" and offered to shake hands with him. The three were preachers that Uncle Dave had known for a good many years, Hanna wrote. Two of them were Baptists, and the other was a Methodist. According to Hanna's recollection, the meeting being held in the brush was less than two miles from Uncle Dave Williams farm on the banks of Cottonwood Creek.

"I venture to say that religion must have been running at a rather low web in and around the Cottonwood Pond settlements. At the Old Mesquite meeting place there was an old log house used for school and church meetings with a big brush arbor near the pond. The three preachers that Uncle Dave met down in the thickets holding some sort of meeting they would not want to hold at their respective meeting places.

"There seemed to have been some sort of quarrel between

70

the three preachers but at their meeting down by the creek in the brush thickets they were in perfect agreement,"[18] Hanna wrote.

Several preachers were believed to have been members of the mob, and one preacher's son was eventually charged with murder. Everyone was suspicious of their neighbors, their friends and even their church leaders.

[1] Archie Douglas Hanna, Excerpt From Unpublished Memoirs, 1958. Provided to author by Frederica Wyatt, Junction, Texas, 2007.

[2] C. L. Sonnichsen, I'll Die Before I Run, the Story of the Great Feuds of Texas, (New York, NY: Harper and Bros., 1951) p. 168.

[3] Ibid., p. 165.

[4] Hanna, op. cit.

[5] Sonnichsen, op. cit., p. 164.

[6] A. Karmen, "Vigilantism," International Encyclopedia of Social Sciences, (Chicago, IL: Macmillan, 1968).

[7] Hanna, op. cit.

[8] Ibid.

[9] Ibid.

[10] Sonnichsen, op. cit., p. 168.

[11] Laura E. Ethridge, E-mail communication to author, August 26, 2003.

[12] Hanna, op. cit.

[13] Ibid.

[14] Ibid.

[15] Ibid.

[16] Sonnichsen, op. cit., p. 169.

[17] Ibid., Page 169-170.

[18] Hanna, op. cit.

Chapter 8:
Courthouse Gunfight

During mob days, killings and bloodletting was not limited to the brush country or along the banks of the Colorado River, nor were the victims limited to ranchers, farmers, gamblers and suspected horse and cow thieves. Victims also included professional men like lawyers, doctors and educators.

In May 1878, while a jury was considering the facts in a liquor election controversy, a San Saba saloonkeeper named William A. "Bill" Brown was shot and mortally wounded in the courtroom by an attorney, T. G. T. Kendall, a law partner of San Saba County Attorney Spencer S. Brooks.

The court was in recess when the dispute began. Voting against serving liquor was a serious matter during frontier days. Tragically, county attorney Brooks also would be gunned down from ambush some four months later apparently in retaliation for the saloonkeeper's death.

About the time that Brooks was appointed county attorney, an election had been held earlier to prohibit the sale of liquor in San Saba County or in a portion of it, according to research conducted in 2002 by David M. Williams, the current county attorney, for a paper presented to the Edwards Plateau Historical Association. Williams, using old court records, newspaper archives and county historical commission papers, observed that a prohibition movement had developed throughout the southwest as a result of the Women's Crusade of 1873 which was a direct action against the saloon business and liquor consumption.

"During this period women had no direct political power but greatly influenced others through 'prayer vigils, petition campaigns, demonstrations, and hymn singing,'" Williams wrote.[1]

By 1877, the town of San Saba had several saloons, primarily operated by Willey Williams and W. A. Brown, and several other merchants had tasting rooms in the rear of their businesses. In addition to drunkenness, Williams observed, many in the community objected to reported gambling, prostitution, and lawless behavior like shooting off their pistols and getting into fistfights.

"One can imagine that San Saba voters in late 1877 were probably influenced by some great church revival to turn away from liquor consumption; however, the vote was rightly contested in court," Williams writes.

There apparently was plenty of animosity between the liquor merchants and the prohibitionists. Some believed that attorney Kendall, Brooks' law partner, had appeared in San Saba about the time that the local option controversy developed and that he was serving as lead defense counsel and also was a noted activist for Prohibition. There also was speculation that Kendall's presence in the county might have carried "hidden agendas."

The courthouse gunfight is perhaps one of the best-documented shootings ever staged in Texas. All the sworn statements of all the surviving eyewitnesses to the incident, including that of lawyer Brooks, have been preserved in the handwritten transcript of a habeas corpus hearing for T.G. T. Kendall taken before E.B. Turner, judge of the 16th Judicial District Court of Travis County in Austin, Texas on June 18, 1878.[2]

While the jury was deliberating the liquor case and the court was in recess, Brown reportedly started to bully the officers of the court. There was no bailiff or sheriff present, so Brown sat in the judge's chair and made statements that should have placed him in contempt of court. Williams said hearing testimony showed that Brown used a cane to bait Brooks and then ordered a sack of liquor to be brought into the courtroom. Williams speculated that Brown was perhaps intoxicated.

When the liquor arrived, Brown invited Brooks to have a drink, but the attorney refused. He also refused Brown's invitation to smoke a cigar, saying that both acts were not appropriate in the courthouse.

Brown kept up hurling insults at Brooks, obviously attempting to goad the attorney into a gunfight. Another attorney, Dan Triplett, attempted to stop the dispute and stepped between the two men. Meanwhile, Kendall stepped outside the courtroom to seek assistance.

When Brown drew his pistol and cocked it, Brooks scrambled for his office while Triplett begged to get out of the way. It was obvious that the dispute had developed into a serious situation.

According to Kendall, Brown was aiming to shoot in Brooks' direction and he asked him to quit. It was too late. Brown fired four shots with his weapon. Kendall, also armed with a pistol, fired twice. One bullet hit Brown in the body and the other bullet was lodged in a door facing, Triplett testified.

Another witness, L. A. Doran, testified that he found Kendall standing at the head of second floor stairway with a pistol in his hand, and Brown was on the floor to the right of the courtroom doorway and about eight feet from the entry to Brooks office.

"Brown reached around my legs with both of his arms and told me he was killed. Brown said I suppose you know who killed me, and I told him I supposed I did. He said Kendall had killed him; said Kendall had shot him in the back, and for me to tell his brother Jim that Kendall had killed him and how he had died," Doran testified.[3]

The shooting of Brown created much excitement in the community, especially among the local saloon trade which had formed a lynching party to revenge their colleague's death. Meanwhile, both Brooks and Kendall remained in the courthouse for their safety, but both were charged with murder the following day. After hearing evidence, the district attorney,

75

F. D. Wilkes, and the county judge discharged Brooks. Kendall admitted probable cause in the Brown's death, and was ordered to be taken to jail in Austin for safekeeping. The judge ordered that Kendall be escorted to the Travis County Jail in Austin by the sheriff who was instructed to "summon a posse of twenty-five men and have them well armed to act as a guard in conveying the prisoner."[4]

According to Williams, the reason for taking Kendall to the Austin jail was twofold: a local mob of saloon operators and their followers gathered and threatened to take Kendall from the San Saba sheriff's custody and lynch him, and the dead man's brother, James Madison Brown, would probably seek revenge.

Ironically, James Madison Brown was then serving as sheriff of Lee County. He had a reputation of being a gambler and being involved in horse racing, and reportedly had killed some 14 men while in office. He would later be killed in a gunfight at Garfield Park in Chicago when police tried to arrest him on a murder warrant from Texas. Two Chicago police officers also were killed in the fracas.

At the time of his death, saloonkeeper Brown was 30 years old, and had been in trouble before. He was the son of John H. "Shorty" Brown, an early day settler in the San Saba area. Brown had been charged earlier in the year with simple assault along with two other men, and also had been charged along with others with selling liquor illegally.

Apparently the liquor situation in 1878 had been creating lots of problems because a Texas Rangers detachment under Lt. George Arrington was sent into the area to maintain order. The adjutant general, in his annual report, noted that there was "strong indications of mob law" developing in the vicinity, and the courtroom shootout just added fuel to the fire.

The presence of the rangers in number made residents feel safer – for a short while anyway.

Texas Ranger James B. Gillett, in his autobiography,

recalled that when the time came to take Kendall to the Travis County Jail in Austin, a large crowd had gathered to see the prisoner. Jim Brown, the Lee County sheriff and brother of Bill Brown, was just a short distance away from the jail doorway, sitting astride his horse and heavily armed with a pistol and Winchester rifle. Gillett's lieutenant, Ranger Nelson Reynolds, ordered the crowd to fall back 50 feet from the hack that would be used to transport Kendall to Austin. Most obeyed the order, but Brown sat perfectly still on his horse. Reynolds quickly ordered his rangers to draw their weapons. The crowd quickly dispersed, but Brown told Reynolds that he was going to ride along with the rangers taking Kendall to Austin.

"If you do, you will go in irons. Move back," the ranger replied. Brown turned his horse and rode away.

According to Williams' research, Brown later told Ranger Reynolds that he had intended to kill Kendall, but he quickly changed his mind when he saw the armed rangers. The ranger said he anticipated Brown attempting to take revenge, thus he had instructed his men "to shoot Brown into doll rags at his first move."[5]

When Brown was unable to put Kendall away, he turned his attention to Brooks. Williams says Brown's motive for killing Brooks was to eliminate "the most favorable witness" for Kendall's defense.

James Madison Brown had an interesting background, Williams found as he put together his research project. In 1878, Brown was serving as sheriff of Lee County, Texas. The county had been carved out of Washington County in 1874 and Brown was its second elected sheriff. The area was still on the Texas frontier and needed strong law enforcement officials. Brown was just the man for the job. He had established himself as a gambler and a racehorse enthusiast and had associated with many lawless persons, including Phillip Houston Coe, John Wesley Hardin and William Preston Longley. Coe became famous because he was the last man killed in a gunfight with James B. (Wild Bill) Hickok. The dispute was said to be over a woman. Hardin, like Brown, liked to gamble at cards, so they crossed trails a number of times. Longley, also a gambler and notorious shootist, would be hanged by Sheriff Brown before a crowd of hundreds at Giddings on October 11, 1878.

Williams noted in his research project that Brown was not opposed to violating his oath of office by getting involved in personal feuds and disputes. He reportedly killed some 14 men while serving in office. Before his violent death in Chicago, he had accumulated a number of racing stables, located about the country, including some in St. Louis, Nashville and Chicago.

Brown would die of gunshot wounds on September 6, 1892, at Garfield Park in Chicago when police attempted to arrest him on an old murder charge filed in Texas. When Brown resisted, he was killed in a gunfight with Chicago police. Two police officers also were slain in the affray.

Stories about the gun battle filled the pages of several Chicago newspapers. One described Brown as a millionaire, but there was no proof of the claim. Some theorized that Brown escaped prosecution in Texas because of his reputation and that he had too many friends that would protect him. He was buried in Fort Worth, where he had relocated his wife and five children. Two of his children, a son and daughter, also would die violently.

According to a story that appeared in the May 11, 1905 issue of the *San Saba News,* Brown's daughter, Annie Stoffer, was shot to death by a man named Fred Street of Fort Worth. Street turned the weapon upon himself after killing the woman, apparently after she refused to live with him. The newspaper described the woman as "something over 25 years of age, and she was of a quiet, retiring disposition."

A son, Gayland Brown, was killed earlier in New Orleans when he was run down by a railroad locomotive.

The gambler turned sheriff also was suspected to be the killer of lawyer S.S. Brooks, who died of an assassin's bullets about four months after Kendall shot Brown's brother in the San Saba County Courthouse. His motive for killing Brooks was to eliminate the most favorable witness for Kendall's defense.

The Brooks killing was called "heart sickening" by District Judge W. A. Blackburn, who examined Brooks and gave him his license to practice law in San Saba.

Brooks was ambushed on Monday evening, September 16, 1878, while walking west on Wallace Street in San Saba. He had left the courthouse a short time earlier to go to the J. C. Montgomery home where he rented a room. When he was about halfway home, he heard someone call out his name. He turned to see who called, and was immediately fired at by James Madison Brown and two other men who Brooks did not recognize.

The seriously injured Brooks, hit by three bullets in his right arm, left shoulder and through the body, fled for safety in the nearby home of Richard Halden, a local gunsmith. According to witnesses, Brooks ran through Haldens house and collapsed in a rear room. The three suspected gunmen also fled the scene.

Brooks, realizing he would soon die of his wounds, asked persons who came to his assistance to summon someone who could take down his dying declaration. While physicians examined his wounds, he dictated to District Clerk W. A. Wilson a detailed statement in lawyerly form:

"To the best of my knowledge and belief it was Jim Brown that shot me," Brooks said.[6]

In a story that appeared in the local newspaper, it was reported that Brooks stated it was Brown who had called out to him as he walked down the street.

Brooks died about 4 a.m. the next morning and was buried the next day in an unmarked grave in Hillcrest

Cemetery, which no longer exists. Its original site is now beneath Rogan Field, a San Saba school athletic facility.

In his presentation, Williams noted that none of Brooks' assailants were ever charged with the murder of the attorney, typical of those violent times when frontier justice reigned throughout the Texas heartland.

Both before and during the Civil War, residents of the Central Texas region experienced from time to time extreme uncertainty and hardship, Williams observed. San Saba County, then only a few years old as an organized county when Texas seceded from the Union, offered little in terms of law enforcement to settlers.

Pioneers were left on the edge of the frontier that was no longer protected by the U.S. Army, thus a frontier guard of old men and boys was organized to help keep hostile Indians under control. As a result, fellow American immigrants wreaked havoc on one another for different reasons and vendetta justice led to mob lawlessness.

County Attorney Williams, in his lengthy research paper, noted that, "by the time that the Brooks homicide could have been investigated and tried, the law enforcement and criminal justice systems for San Saba County were in shambles."[7]

County Sheriff W. R. Doran, in office about the time of the Brooks killing, was under indictment by a local grand jury for taking a bribe and for unlawfully dealing in county script, and there were tensions between the sheriff and other officers of the court. The bribery charges were later dismissed, but Doran lost his job when a deputy, Gus Loftin, was elected sheriff in November 1878.

The killing of Brooks and the courtroom shooting of Brown was mostly forgotten until March 1, 1890, when an attempt to kill T.G.T. Kendall was allegedly made by James Madison Brown while Kendall and his son rode in a buggy near Kendall's home just off Swiss Avenue in Dallas. The shot missed its intended mark but wounded Kendall in the upper leg. Brown was suspected to be the shooter. He was then living with his family in Fort Worth and many persons remembered that the Brown faction in San Saba County had sworn vengeance on Kendall for the 1879 shooting of Billy Brown in the courthouse.

[1] David M. Williams, "The Vicious Murder of S. S. Brooks," Historical Paper presented to the Edwards Plateau Historical Association, October 5, 2002, San Saba, Texas, p. 5.

[2] Ibid., p. 6.

[3] Ibid., Appendix C, p. ii

[4] Ibid., p. 7.

[5] Ibid., p. 8.

[6] Ibid., p. 1.

[7] Ibid., p. 4.

Chapter 9:
"Bob War" Caused Some Violence

"A serious drought in the spring and summer of 1883 was a clarion call that times were changing," stated noted historian Roy D. Holt in a story written in December 1938 for the *Cattleman Magazine,* the official publication of the Texas and Southwestern Cattle Raisers Association. Holt, a part time writer and full time school administrator who served several West Texas communities over the years, pointed out that there was no more free grass for livestock to eat and no more readily available water for them to drink. Trails and roads and open range were now barricaded by new barbed wire.

A herd of Texas Longhorns, like those that ran wild in frontier Texas, graze and rest in a West Texas pasture. Millions of these kind of animals were trailed to the Midwest markets after the Civil War. Photo courtesy of the Livestock Weekly, San Angelo, Texas.

As a result, gangs roamed the Texas Heartland with a new weapon – wire nippers – and fences were being cut in numerous counties.

In Hamilton County, a mob of 15 men left a drawing of a coffin and a note to a landowner after cutting his barbed wire fence around a pasture. The note indicated they were determined to have free grass and water. At another location, fence cutters left a note with a bullet hole in it. The note read, "If you don't make gates, we will make them for you.[1]

Fence cutting was not limited to being a problem for cattlemen. With the coming of sheep flocks to Central Texas, a conflict quickly developed into open hostilities between cowmen and sheepherders in some locations, says noted sheep industry historian Edward N. Wentworth in his now out-of-print book, *America's Sheep Trails,* published in 1948 by Iowa State College Press.

According to Wentworth, the Civil War accentuated the conflict of interest between the sheepmen and cattlemen in Texas. Even before the war began, cattlemen were of the opinion that herding sheep was no job for a "white" man, still associating sheep raising with Mexicans after Texans took over cattle ranching.[2]

With the growth of immigration among Europeans, particularly of English and German settlers coming to Texas, sheep became an important source of income on farms.

Wentworth notes that many of the immigrant families that came to Texas in 1845 with Prince de Solms to settle in the Texas Hill Country projected themselves into the sheep industry, and even before hostilities broke out in the Civil War sheep raisers had spread into the area around Boerne and were there when Kendall County was organized in 1862. As a result, flocks of sheep and their immigrant owners were soon moving west along the Guadalupe River, settling in the 1860s and 1870s in the area now marked by Guadalupe, Gillespie, Comal, Fayette, Washington, Colorado, Austin, Mason, Kendall,

Kimble, Kerr, Blanco and San Saba counties.[3]

In his book, *Cattlemen vs. Sheepherders, Five Decades of Violence in the West,* published in 1989 by Eakin Press, author-historian Bill O'Neal reports that during a two-month time starting in December 1879, there were a number of raids against San Saba County sheep camps. One sheepherder, Peter Bertrand, was ordered out of the county by a band of riders, and a dog was brought along to attack Bertrand's sheep. When the man tried to stay in the county, nightriders shot his sheep while they were penned for the night.

According to O'Neal, the worst attack on sheepmen happened on January 12, 1880, when a raid was made on the Ramsey Brothers.

The Ramseys owned 7,000 sheep that they ranged in south San Saba County and just across the line in adjacent Llano County. One band of 1,300 sheep was pastured at Fall Creek Prairie, located in lower San Saba County, where a herder named Colvin kept them penned at night while he camped a short distance away. When the raiders came upon his camp, he did not offer any resistance.

The mob dismounted, entered the pens and commenced to slit the throats of the bleating animals. When the mob members tired of their bloody work, they opened the gates and scattered the surviving sheep, leaving 240 head dead and numerous others seriously injured.

Author O'Neal also related stories of similar acts of violence in Coleman, Hamilton and other counties. In reaction to these events and others, the editor of the publication, *Texas Wool,* observed: "In almost every case the aggressors have been the cattlemen."

"The mission of barbed wire on earth seems to be to create trouble. Here and in neighboring states barbed wire is monopolizing the attention of courts and lawyers, and down here in Texas it is killing cowboys and peace officers all over the prairies...Dynamite distresses England; barbed wire is what hurts us," declared an editorial that appeared in the May 6, 1884, issue of the *Texas Stockman,* published in San Antonio.

In 1875, barbed wire was brought into Texas and gradually cattlemen started using the wire as a cheap way to enclose large tracts of land. Smaller landowners also started using the wire to fence their farms. In just a few years time, fencing helped push the frontier of Texas farther westward than it had during the previous 50 years.

Land that had been utilized by Texas stockmen in common for many years was suddenly surrounded by a shiny new barrier that had sharp barbs on it. Not only was land enclosed by the wire, so were streams, waterholes and ponds which had been previously free to all. What made matters even worse was finding fence wire stretched across roadways that also had been open to travelers so long that most considered the roads public property.

Settlers in Texas had become so accustomed to looking out for themselves during the 1870s and 1880s that they did not pause a moment to think about what to do when faced with wire barriers. They simply cut the fence.

It is not known just when the first fence was cut in Texas, but it spread rapidly. By 1882, stories about fence cutting were appearing in national newspapers. The *Chicago Drovers Journal* was quoted as saying that the original fence cutter was one of Texas's most famous Indian fighters, Big Foot Wallace, who cut wire in Frio County on land owned by the Hawkeye Cattle Company.[4]

Fence cutting was becoming such a problem by 1883 that the Adjutant General of Texas, W. H. King, made a personal visit to the north and northwestern portions of the state to determine just how widespread the practice had become.

The *Texas Livestock Journal,* in March 1883, reported that in some southern counties of the state gangs of men had shown "great aversion" to fence wire because it "interfered" with their business.[5]

85

In August 1883, a correspondent for the *Fort Worth Gazette* noted that, "there is scarcely a large pasture in this entire country that has not been summarily opened and in some instances many miles of wire have been cut, literally shaved to pieces. And to complete the wreck, oftentimes the posts are pulled up and burned."

Because of the severe drought that gripped the state in the summer of 1883, it was reported that cattle in the west were dying of thirst so fences were cut to allow them access to water.

The drought was just one of the causes for fence cutting, but in many cases this was no justification for the lawlessness that was breaking out all over the Texas Heartland. In November 1883, the *Austin Statesman reported* that once the lawlessness started, it rapidly spread into an epidemic. Rail fences, constructed of wood poles cut from native tree stands, were burned, sheep were killed and herders were beaten and whipped.

Another cause of fence cutting was stockmen's desire for free grass. If all the wire fences could be destroyed the range would be open again, which some stock raisers believed that Texas had become great under the open range system.

"Free grass is the shibboleth, and woe be unto the unlucky wight (person) who cannot glibly pronounce the mystic word," wrote a Cass County correspondent in the *Fort Worth Daily Gazette.* (Note: For readers without a Webster's dictionary, the word, shibboleth, a noun, means a long standing belief or principle held by a group of people.)

W. J. Davis of Hamilton County was one of many who had his pasture fence cut. However, a note was left tacked on one of the few fence posts left standing. The note, with the picture of a coffin on it, stated: "This to the wire fence men: We want free grass and water, and free grass and water we are going to have at the risk of our own lives and property. Thers (there's) 15 sens (signs) this."[6]

Another cause of the fence cutting during the 1880s revolved around the closing of roads by newly stretched wire with no gates. Texans had been accustomed "to traveling through; not around," said one old timer. The *Mobeetie Panhandle* newspaper observed that cattlemen were committing a grave error in not putting a sufficient number of gates along the lines of their fences.

Fence cutting was not limited to just open range cattlemen. An Army officer caused considerable trouble for the government, as well as himself, when he ordered one of his troopers to cut a fence that was across the regular road. While the troopers were cutting the fence, the landowner rode up and threatened to have the officer indicted. The officer said the indictment would be decided by who filed the charge first.

The cavalry detachment proceeded to go into the county seat where the officer filed a complaint against the landowner for blocking the roadway. The landowner was soon found guilty of obstructing a public road and fined. The judge turned over a portion of the fine to the officer who gave the money to local churches. When he returned to his station at Fort Elliott, he found a gallon of good whiskey on hand for himself and his detachment. The spirits did not come from church members.[7]

In the March 30, 1884 issue of the *San Antonio Express,* a correspondent noted that one of the frequent reasons given for fence cutting was that large areas of land were being enclosed by fences controlled by joint-stock companies or corporations whose stockholders were foreigners, particularly English and Scottish citizens of wealth.

"Principalities and aphasics have been created among a few capitalists which has aroused a spirit of agrarianism among the poorer classes," the story stated.

Who were these fence cutters that were creating such havoc? Historian Holt says that among the first groups to oppose the wholesale fencing of the range were the cowboys, who saw their jobs threatened.

Under the pasture system, Holt explained, one man could do the work of five men on the open range. The cowboys opposed the wire fence just as a laborer was opposed to machines.[8]

Under the system of fencing first and leasing or buying later, lands owned by the State of Texas were particularly vulnerable to illegal occupancy. By the time the fence cutters started working, there were thousands of acres of public land that had been illegally enclosed so it was in protest against this kind of fencing that led to wire cutting and ultimately violence.

One of the most unfortunate aspects of the fence wars was the formation of reckless gangs of men organized to destroy fences. Such gangs or mobs were generally composed of "almost entirely of the outlaw element."[9]

A certain bunch operating in Central Texas called themselves "Mob No. 1. Others operating to the south called themselves "the Blue Devils" and "the Javelinas."[10]

Fence cutters were hard to identify and even more difficult to catch. They carried no loot, worked mostly at night, often wore masks and many did not carry weapons. Their tools of trade were nippers or pliers and they rarely left a trail to follow. The late Walter P. Webb, chronicler of the Texas Rangers, observed that the "fence cutter carried no evidence of his deed...he had to be caught on the job."

By the fall of 1883, damage from fence cutting in Texas was estimated at some $20 million – at more than $1 million in Brown County alone. It had gotten so bad that the *Fort Worth Gazette* estimated that tax valuations had declined by $30 million, and that the clashes between the mobs and ranchers was scaring away prospective settlers. Politicians at the time shied from the issue.[11]

Texas Governor John Ireland called a special session of the Texas Legislature on October 15, 1883, to meet on January 8, 1884.

After a lengthy session, highlighted by a deluge of

petitions and heated debates, the legislators approved a bill making fence cutting a felony punishable by a prison sentence of one to five years. The penalty for malicious pasture burning was two to five years in the prison. The fencing of public lands or of lands belonging to others knowingly and without permission was made a misdemeanor, and builders of such fencing were required to remove them within a six months period. Ranchers who built a fence across a public road were required to place a gate every three miles and to keep the gates in good repair.[12]

However, fence cutting was not totally stopped, particularly in Brown County where mobs of armed fence cutters had taken shots at landowners attempting to protect their property. In 1886, several years after the Texas Legislature made fence cutting a felony, two fence cutters were shot dead by Texas Rangers one night on the Baugh Ranch near Jim Ned Creek.

During a time of intense excitement when fence cutters threatened to burn the town of Brownwood, armed men patrolled the streets every night, recalled the late Will H. Mayes, the first dean of the School of Journalism at the University of Texas in Austin, in an interview with historian Holt in 1936.

During the fence cutting wars, Mayes was a 22-year-old lawyer who served as Brown County attorney. The measures passed by the Legislature eventually ended most of the troubles, although there were sporadic outbreaks of nipping fences for the next decade, especially during droughts. Texas Rangers were sent to stop fence cutters in Navarro County in 1888, and they later made several cases in West Texas for a few more years.[13]

---

[1] Paul H. Carlson, Texas Woollybacks, The Range Sheep And Goat Industry, (College Station, TX: Texas A&M University Press, College Station, 1982) p. 185.

[2] Edward N. Wentworth, America's Sheep Trails, (Ames, IA: Iowa State College Press, 1948) p. 384.

[3] Ibid., p. 385.

[4] R.D. Holt, The Cattleman Magazine, December 1938, p. 33.

[5] Ibid., p. 33.

[6] Ibid., p. 36.

[7] Ibid., p. 37.

[8] Ibid., p. 39.

[9] Henry D. and Frances T. McCallum, The Wire That Fenced The West, (Norman, OK: University of Oklahoma Press, 1985) p. 161.

[10] Ibid., p. 161-162.

[11] "Fence Cutting," The Handbook of Texas Online, <http://www.tshaonline.org/handbook/online/>

[12] Ibid.

[13] Ibid.

Chapter 10:
Last Bite Of Cake

A slice of cake was the last thing Dee Edmondson saw before a shotgun blast roared through a knocked out kitchen window, splintering the window facing and burying eight buckshot in his body from the belt up.

This was how the late Mason cowboy, Gene "Sie" Banta, recalled Edmondson's death by an alleged mob assassin while he and several other men prepared to eat a late evening snack after being on a fishing trip and playing baseball at Voca that evening.

Banta wrote about the murder in his memoirs, *"20 Years A Buckaroo,"* written before he died in 1959. Laid up with asthma in 1953, Banta used his time at home to start writing down his recollections in longhand. The book was later published by Banta's son, Charles Banta of Mason, in collaboration with the Mason County Historical Commission.

According to Banta's recollections, there were five cowboys in the group that rode to a place in Long Valley where they were to clean and cook their fish, and spend the night.

After putting their horses in the corral, feeding and watering them, the young cowhands put their saddles on the back porch of the house. A bunch of hounds greeted them when they rode up.

In his memoirs, Banta recalled that there was a smoke house behind the house that had a window. There also was an eight-inch strip that had been knocked out of the door next to the kitchen.

"We were all sitting around eating fish except Dee," Banta wrote. "He had a plate in his hand and walked to the safe near the open kitchen door, pulled the safe open and turned and asked Will (Edmondson) if he ate all the cake, and Will said no. Dee said, I see you didn't. That was the last words he ever spoke."[1]

Banta recalled that he was sitting almost in line with Dee Edmondson when he was thrust into eternity by a shotgun blast.

"The blast almost blinded me …whoever it was fired the shot put the shotgun through the back window, missed the strip that was knocked out of the door, and nine buckshot went through one inch thick soft pine. Eight shots (pellets) hit him from the belt up and one lodged in the door facing and knocked my face full of splinters and pieces of plate," Banta wrote.[2]

Banta said the mortally wounded man sat down, and then fell over. The man's brother, Will, quickly went to him and tried to pick him up.

"Then I seen some blood on his breast. None of us stayed in that kitchen," Banta continued.[3]

In the excitement following the shooting, Banta said the cowboys were terrified and sought their Winchesters and six-shooters for protection. They also ran to the corral for their horses in order to spread the alarm. The shooter escaped during the commotion.

Banta and William Taylor were the first men to reach the corral. They mounted their horses bareback and left in a run for Uncle Gus Liverman's place about a mile away.

"We stopped there long enough to tell him (about the shooting), grab a saddle and light out for Voca," Banta wrote. Voca, a small McCulloch County community, was seven miles away.

Banta recalled that Sheriff Jim Wall was summoned to investigate the shooting, along with some deputies and a justice of the peace, serving as a coroner, who held an inquest.

"The next morning, none of us boys could tell the same tale and it is still a mystery," Banta commented.

The Dee Edmondson murder was not the only act of suspected mob violence in McCulloch County or in the vicinity

92

of Voca, according to the late Wayne Spiller, who worked for years compiling a three-volume history of the county. Spiller was a rancher in the Voca community for many years.

One of the first mob victims was a man named J. Y. Criswell, who was shot from his wagon and killed instantly near his home on August 9, 1888.

According to Spiller, the Deep Creek area holds many lurid and dismal secrets because several shootings occurred there as settlers came in droves after 1875, including many squatters. In addition to Criswell being ambushed, Doss White had been killed a short time earlier and Ed Millholland had died of a reported accidental shooting.

Criswell, called Yank, was a pioneer resident of Deep Creek, which now comprise the communities of Cowboy and Round Mountain. No one was ever charged with the murder, and he was buried in the Cowboy community cemetery, located in the northeast corner of the county near the Colorado River. Spiller wrote that his research into events of the time revealed that, "the captain of the mob in McCulloch (County) resided at Voca."[4]

"Unlike many modern, secret terrorist groups, the mob never took credit for eliminating its enemies. It was left to the general public to draw its own conclusions. It is, therefore, possible that the mob was blamed for some murders it did not commit," Spiller observed.[5]

In his commentary about the mob, Spiller said three McCulloch County men, including Sheriff F. M. "Buck" Miller, Jim Longley and County Attorney L. C. Matthis, were each marked for execution but all survived.

Longley was the man selected by the mob to eliminate Miller, but he refused the order because Miller was a close friend and he immediately defected from the mob. A short time later, Spiller wrote, Longley was shot from ambush, the bullet knocking him down and burning a bloody crease across the back of his neck.

Matthis, a Sunday School superintendent at the Methodist church, was almost a witness to a mob execution in neighboring San Saba County in August, 1893.

Having become a Methodist minister, he was on that warm night in August holding a revival meeting at China Knob, some four miles north of San Saba. After the service, Spiller wrote, some three-quarters of a mile distant from the church, Jim Brown, traveling with a group on the way home from the services, was killed by a load of buckshot fired from a shotgun.[6]

A Voca man, George Brown, no relation to the San Saba victim, was assassinated on the night of January 4, 1893. His body was discovered the following day, hanging from an oak tree limb, the feet almost touching the ground.

"The site of this violence, four miles out from Brady on the Voca road, was pointed out to the compiler in his early youth," Spiller wrote. "The tree stood about 225 yards north of Four Mile Draw on the east side of the road just before the road made a 90 degree turn to the west."[7]

Another McCulloch County man to die violently apparently at the hands of a mob was a Mr. Bradley who was shot from his horse in 1893 in the north central portion of the county. A son of Mr. Bradley told writer Spiller in 1966 that his father's murderer got religious in later years and confessed to the crime. When the son learned the man's identity, he made plans to kill him but was dissuaded by his mother.[8]

Like families in many of the counties in the Texas Heartland, McCulloch folks chose to vacate and relocate when their names were linked by local gossip to mob activities.

Mason cowboy Banta explained the peoples' nervousness this way:

"I lived with Uncle Gus (Liverman) for a while and would go all over the county to dances and parties, but when I came home late I would have a pistol in my hand, still scared almost to death, and when it got dark I would get off (the horse) in the dark; never went where there was a light."[9]

[1]Eugene Mardell Banta, <u>20 Years A Buckaroo</u>, (Ozark, MO: Dogwood Printing Inc., 2007) p. 8.

[2] Ibid., p. 8.

[3]Ibid., p. 8.

[4]Wayne Spiller, <u>Handbook of McCulloch County History, Volume II</u>, (Brady, TX: Heart of Texas Historical Museum, 1984) p. 18.

[5] Ibid., p. 18.

[6] Ibid., p. 19.

[7] Ibid., p. 19.

[8] Ibid., p. 19.

[9] Banta, op. cit., p. 9.

Chapter 11:
Horse Stealing: A Hanging Offense

The year 1883 was not a happy time for settlers in Hamilton County. Horses were disappearing, despite the fact that the county had been considered rather free from horse stealing until that time.

"Not much was thought about it at first," recalled Cecil B. James in writing his recollections of that time for a history of the county archived in the Texas Collection at Baylor University. "There were few fences, and horses would stray some distance. As the number of missing horses increased, people began looking for clues."

According to James' story, folks started to notice that a man named Garrison always kept several horses in his lot, yet he farmed very little and did not have many cattle to care for.

Folks began to notice that he would have a different number of animals that had a different appearance, and that the man did not attend the "stray sale day" when unidentified animals would be sold. James said it quickly became evident that Garrison was operating a "way station" for a ring of horse thieves operating in other counties. When this evidence was given to the Hamilton County sheriff, Garrison was arrested and lodged in the county jail where he was held in a steel cage located on the second floor.

According to writer James, the jail at that time was at the north end of a lot later occupied by a department store. The jail was two stories in height, constructed of native rock, with a steel cage on the top floor.

The suspected horse thief, Garrison, had been in jail for awhile when a rumor circulated through the town that a gang of his friends were going to rescue him from the jail. The sheriff, not taking any chance of losing his prisoner, hired extra guards to watch the jail at night.

On a moonlit night in August 1884, a large group of men, wearing long slickers and carrying Winchester rifles, galloped into town.

"With military precision, they tied their horses to the courthouse fence and took up stations around the town," James wrote. "When the guards were confronted by the others, they knew they could not hold out so they locked everything and pitched the key into the well."

According to James' story, Garrison thought that the mounted men were his friends coming to get him out of jail, so he gave them encouragement. When the men could not find a key to unlock the steel cage, several men went to the Miller and Streepy Blacksmith Shop where they got sledgehammers and pry bars and began breaking the cage door open. The noise awakened many people in town. James' father stepped outside to see what was happening. One of the men on guard immediately stepped up to him and told him "to step back inside that door." When he hesitated, another man yelled, "put a bullet hole through him." James' father quickly went inside. Several other men also were stopped by the guards posted by the mob, including Judge Goodson and a Judge Eidson. James did not identify which court the men presided over.

Garrison, happy being released from jail, did not realize that the men meant to harm him. He was quickly hurried just north of the square to the Graves pasture where a large oak tree stood near the southwest corner of the cemetery. He was pleading for his life when the men tossed the rope over a tree limb and pulled him up until his feet were about five feet from the ground. He strangled to death.

After about 15 minutes, the executioners returned to the courthouse, called in the patrols, mounted their horses and quietly rode away. Tragically, Garrison's wife drove into town the next morning in her buggy with a fresh change of clothing for her husband. Only then did she learn what happened to her husband the night before.

According to James, no grand jury action was taken because most of the men were out of the county, thus members of the mob were never identified.[1]

Coryell County, which joins Hamilton County on the southeast, also had its problems with mobs and violence, which started in 1865.

During the Civil War, there was a character named Frank Horko who lived in the county. He got into a lot of trouble with his neighbors when he refused to serve in the Confederate Army or as a ranger helping to protect the frontier from the Indians.

As a result of his refusal to serve as a volunteer and being ostracized by his neighbors, he started raiding the settlements, stealing horses and cattle. The settlers tried to catch Horko, but he moved into the western part of the county that was poorly settled, built a cabin on one of the ranches and joined a small band of Indians.

A posse of rangers located Horko near his cabin, but he quickly mounted his horse and fled into the brush, escaping capture. A man named Alfred Kerby was among the rangers and tried to overtake Horko, but Kerby was riding a horse that he had just unhitched from a plow a few days earlier. The horse, out of condition for running, could not keep up with Horko's mount and Kerby was unable to get within gunshot range.[2]

Later, during a scout of King's Mountain in 1865, a plume of smoke was seen rising out of the timber on a branch to the east. A ranger scout was able to get close enough to the camp to recognize Horko and some of his Indian companions. Coryell County Sheriff J. C. Haynes was contacted in Gatesville, and a posse was formed. The lawman was able to capture and arrest Horko and return him to the county jail in Gatesville.

Settlers in the area, disgusted with the time it took to

bring Horko to justice, did not propose risking Horko's escape. That night, a mob surrounded the jail, took Horko out of his cell to a live oak tree just outside of town and hanged him. Settler justice was swift, no one was charged with the jail assault or with the lynching of Horko.[3]

Coryell County was organized in 1854, created from Bell County, and named for early pioneer settler James Coryell.[4]

In those days, Gatesville had 10 liquor saloons, and it was a time of mob violence – not the lynching of Negroes, for there were few Negroes in the county – but the lynching of white men who happened to know too much concerning a fellow criminal, or who had fallen in disfavor with the ruling lights of mobdom, according to an editorial written by J. B. Cranfill, editor of the *Gatesville Messenger and Star-Forum,* on December 15, 1939.[5]

The hanging of Horko did not stop outlawry, says historian Frank Simmons. "Brigands infested the country for years until the life of no man or his livestock were safe. During this period, a trio of men, including Rueben Queen, Bill Leverett and Andy Wolff, conceived the idea of not waiting for the law for protection, for the law enforcement authorities were helpless. They, with others, banded themselves together under a bond to allow no outlaw to escape once sighted."[6]

In December 1889, while returning to Gatesville with a wagon load of supplies, John T. Matthes and W.H. Harvey were held up and robbed on the Lampasas Road about 12 miles southwest of Gatesville. Matthes was shot during the holdup and his companion, Harvey, was seriously wounded. Matthes would die about 36 hours after the robbery. On the day of the robbery, a man named Bob Wells met two men near the crime scene, and the wounded Harvey sent word to the sheriff that two men named Jim Leeper and Ed Powell were responsible. When Wells saw Leeper on the street in Gatesville, he pointed him out to lawmen that quickly arrested him. Leeper, on being taken to jail, told officers that his companion, Powell, could be found at the Buster place near Turnerville. Sheriff Lanham quickly organized another posse and went to Turnerville where he found Powell in bed, having suffered a blow to the head when teamster Harvey whacked him with the butt end of an ox whip.[7]

According to writer Zelma Scott, the examining trial did not take very long. Leeper and Powell were both charged with murder in the first degree, and the case was set for trial on February 6, 1890.

Although defense attorney J. L. Crain put up a good argument for a new trial date during the following court term, his motion was overruled. The men were found guilty and given the death penalty. However, an appeal was filed with the Court of Criminal Appeals on May 24, 1890, which reaffirmed the lower court's ruling.

On July 23, 1891, both men were sentenced to be hanged in public on Saturday August 29, 1891. However, more court actions delayed the execution. There was an accusation that Powell's mother had tried to bribe the sheriff to leave a key in the jail cell door lock, and a rumor was circulated that there had been jury misconduct. Despite these delays, the hanging was rescheduled for September 29, 1891, at 2 p.m. As the town clock chimed 2 o'clock, Sheriff John Hammack tripped the trap that sent the men to eternity. A large crowd had gathered to see the men hanged on a specially built scaffold.[8]

Several years went by before another murder was reported in the county.

On August 11, 1892, the following story appeared in the *Gatesville Star:*

"Last Saturday night a party of masked men went to the house of a man living on Cowhouse Creek in Coryell County and took him out and gave him a serious whipping with a rope. While the whipping was going on, the man asked why the gang was punishing him, and he was told it was because he would not work his crop and support his family. He was offered work at $1.25 per day, but refused to work. It is said that since that time he has left the county."[9]

Like many other counties located in the Texas Heartland, Coryell County had difficulties establishing law and order. It took special kinds of people to run for sheriff or to serve as a deputy sheriff or city marshal. While many law abiding citizens were arriving to buy farm and ranch land and to establish businesses, it also had its share of outlaws moving through looking for easy herds of cattle or bands of horses to steal. As a result, self-protection of livestock and property was of paramount importance.

As Central Texas area counties struggled to establish law and order, vigilante committees and loosely organized gangs or mobs were organized to rid the counties of the bad elements. Tragically, after the outlaws were run out of the territory or caught and dealt with severely, some of these same law abiding citizens started working on each other as land, property and livestock became coveted by neighbors and others. It was a familiar pattern that was followed in many of the counties.

According to writer Michael Barr, a certain area in southeastern Coryell County became a haven for a bunch of cattle rustlers and horse thieves. He notes that the thick cedar brakes a rough back country along Owl and Cowhouse creeks proved to be nearly a perfect hiding place for stolen livestock.[10]

Barr observes that the unstable environment eventually produced a number of men of questionable character who did not care who "they had to cheat, shoot or rob" to get what they wanted.[11] One in particular was a man named Ed Cash who had a place about 12 miles southeast of Gatesville.

Barr says Cash got away with stealing livestock because people feared him. His neighbors turned a blind eye to his lawless activities as long as he did not covet their stock and did his stealing elsewhere. Cash also apparently had a mean streak and did not mind sending a man to the promised land if confronted.

Cash got into trouble when some of his neighbors animals started to appear in his pens. Not only did Cash's neighbors turn against him, even some of his "acquaintances and relatives by blood and marriage"[12] got tired of his shenanigans. Neighbors got together – secretly – in a secluded place and his fate was sealed. He was taken from his home on a rainy night in April 1894, and hanged from a limb of a big oak tree that was just a short distance from his front porch.

Cash was caught off guard by the mobbers while standing in front of a fireplace, waiting for his wife to give birth in a back room of the house. Dr. Rufus C. Smith, who lived about two miles away, had been summoned earlier that night to deliver the baby.

Cash did not hear the masked men before they rushed into the house because of the wind and rain. Despite Dr. Smith's pleading that Cash be allowed to see his child before being taken away, the mob was in no mood to wait, Barr related.[13] Before mounting up and leaving, each man put a bullet into the dangling corpse.

Cash's lynching was subsequently investigated by the county sheriff, but no charges were ever filed in the case, although the sheriff found horse tracks leading from the hanging tree to several houses located nearby.

In developing his story about the Cash hanging, writer Barr learned that a 16-year-old boy living nearby witnessed the mob's work that night, but when questioned by the sheriff about the crime, the boy could not identify any of the mob. "Perhaps his eyesight was bad. Perhaps he wanted to live to see seventeen," Barr commented.[14]

---

[1] Cecil B. James narrative, published in a book titled "A History of Hamilton County Texas," a copy provided by the Texas Collection, Baylor University Library, Waco.

[2] Frank E. Simmons, History of Coryell County, (Gatesville, TX: Coryell County News, 1936) p. 29-33.

[3] Ibid., p. 29-33.

[4] The Texas Almanac Sesquicentennial Edition,1857-2007, p. 202.

[5] Zelma Scott, A History of Coryell County, (Austin, TX: Texas State Historical Association, 1965) p. 135.

[6] Simmons, op. cit., p. 29-33.

[7] Scott, op. cit., p. 143-145.

[8] Ibid., p. 145.

[9] Ibid., p. 145.

[10] Michael Barr, Rope Burns & Lead Poisoning, The Wild West In Central Texas, (Gatesville, TX: Mikes Books, 2006) p. 19.

[11] Ibid., p. 19.

[12] Ibid., p. 20.

[13] Ibid., p. 21.

[14] Ibid., p. 22.

Chapter 12:
A Most Tragic Incident

Mob violence was not limited to "eliminating" bands of cattle rustlers, horse thieves or cleaning up frontier towns of gamblers and other unsavory characters that sought ways to make money without working.

One of the most tragic incidents ever recorded in the Texas Heartland happened in Blanco County on August 24, 1885, when a man named Albert L. Lackey shot and killed six persons, including members of his own family and relatives. Those murdered were his brother, a daughter, a niece, another relative and Mr. And Mrs. J. C. Stokes, the father and mother-in-law of Green B. Lackey, a brother of Albert.

Lee Brown, a longtime resident of Blanco, reported the story in the *Blanco News*. His account of the brutal murders was published later in the *Frontier Times* magazine in April 1936. According to historian Brown, Albert Lackey saddled his horse and armed with a Winchester rifle, started out to exterminate the entire Lackey connection located along the Pedernales River and Hickory Creek in the north end of the county. Brown observed that Albert Lackey apparently had become mad or demented for some reason before going on his murder rampage.

Riding up the river valley, the first victim was his niece who was sitting near the front door of her home, rocking and singing to her new baby. When the woman's body was found lying on the floor, the baby was asleep against the body covered with its mother's blood.

Lackey's second victim was his brother, unnamed in the story, who ran in an effort to escape harm, but he tripped and fell. As he begged for his life, Lackey stuck the gun behind the brother's ear and pulled the trigger, blowing the man's brains out of his head.

Mr. And Mrs. Stokes, described as an aged couple, were his next victims, dead from bullets fired from Lackey's rifle, and then his own daughter and another relative were slain. When he found that he was out of ammunition, he rode to his own home where he tried to kill his wife and small baby with a knife. However, his wife managed to flee the house with the child in her arms and found a hiding place in a thicket. When Lackey could not find his wife, he slashed his own throat, but she said the wound did not appear to be deep enough to cause Lackey to slow down. He mounted his horse and left his home at a trot, headed in the direction of Johnson City.

On the road, Lackey met a neighbor, Al Bundick, and asked him to ride with him to a nearby spring. Bundick noted that Lackey had a handkerchief around his throat that he believed to be a red bandana. As the men rode toward Johnson City, Lackey got behind Bundick and slashed at the man with his knife, cutting Bundick seriously until he fell from his horse.

When Lackey arrived in Johnson City, he told several people that Bundick had slain some of Lackey's family and had attacked him in which his throat had been cut. A posse was formed to go and search for Bundick, but before the mounted men could leave town, a son of Lackey came into town and told lawmen that his father had killed family members but he did not know how many were dead.

Bundick was found and taken home were a doctor tended his wounds. He was badly cut, but would recover in a few weeks.

Mrs. Lackey told the sheriff of her escape from her deranged husband and seeing him cut his own throat. Lackey was brought to jail after a doctor had sewn up his slashed throat. Although Blanco was the county seat at the time, Lackey was taken to the Johnson City jail and lodged there until he could be removed.

On August 25, 1885, the six members of Lackey's family

were buried in a small cemetery on Hickory Creek, about two miles below where the Sandy Post Office was then located.

Albert Lackey was soon to meet his ultimate judge. On the afternoon of August 26, rancher Charlie Cabaniss was headed for town from his place on Miller Creek just beyond Brushy Top when a large party of men overtook him on the road. The group told him he could wait with them, have an early supper, and then continue into town with them. They ate supper at a spring a few hundred yards below the Miller Creek crossing on present U. S. Highway 281.

Sometime after dark, the group rode quietly into Johnson City, captured the guards before any ruckus developed, and then silently rode to the jail. A few citizens noticed the big bunch of riders, and soon found the mob at the jail.

Phil P. Cage, who recognized several of the riders, told the group that a very sick woman was at home near the jail and asked that no commotion be made. Several members of the mob thought that Cage was trying to stop the lynch party. The leader told them to hush. He knew Cage to be a good man who would not alarm the community. He then led the way to Lackey's cell, told the murderer that they had come for him to pay for his crimes and opened the cell door.

As the door creaked open, Lackey grabbed a large iron bucket that was in the cell and used for waste. He tried to hit the mob leader with the bucket, but it hit the top of the cell and was deflected. Lackey was quickly overpowered and taken to the jail yard. According to historian Moursund and early-day resident Lee Brown, it had been the mob's intention to get to Blanco in the afternoon and have a public execution, hanging Lackey from a limb of a large live oak tree that was still standing at the southwest corner of the old courthouse building a few years ago.

At the request of the man Cage, the mob soon rode north out of town, joined by a number of local citizens, to a site by the road where two large live oak trees were located. One person in the crowd suggested that Lackey be strung up from a limb on the closest tree, but Lackey, who had remained in stoic silence since being loaded into the old wagon at the jail, looked up and said, "the limb is too low and almost over the road."

Another tree nearby was quickly selected, the wagon in which Lackey was seated quickly brought beneath a big limb, and a noose which had been previously tied in a traditional hangman's knot was put around his wounded neck.

Someone hollered that Lackey should be shot because of the deep cut on his throat, but the rope was thrown over the limb and the wagon driven away. Rather than jump from the chair on which he was standing, Lackey was dragged from the wagon by the rope so his neck was not broken. He slowly strangled to death, his body twisting on the rope. When the rope stopped twisting, Lackey's feet almost touched the ground. Another rope was quickly put around his neck and his body raised "quite a distance higher," according to Brown's story.

Finishing their brutal work, the mob rode northward from the town and dispersed. The next morning, August 27, Lewellyn Robinson held a coroner's inquest at the place of the hanging. Lackey was a large man with iron gray hair and mustache. He looked like a terrible and gruesome giant as he swung in the air. The noose had cut deeply into his neck where he had slashed himself. The body was taken down and delivered to John R. Robison who had contracted to bury the man in the southeast corner of the Robison field located about a half-mile northwest of town.[1]

Blanco County, located on the eastern edge of the Edwards Plateau, comprises about 714 square miles. It is generally hilly to mountainous, and has a landscape "stair step" appearance due to limestone benches and steep slopes. There is archeological evidence that Indians camped in the Blanco County area as early as 1150 AD, and ancestors of the Lipan Apaches may have roamed the area when the Spanish arrived in the 16th Century.[2]

Land agents, impresarios and Indian fighters started to drift into the Blanco River country about 1821, but land grants were not issued by the Mexican government until 1826 when Benjamin Milam was given approval to settle 300 families between the Colorado and Guadalupe rivers. Among those receiving land in 1835 were Jesse McCrocklin, Horace Eggleston, Noel Mixson and Ben Williams. Each got a league of land but the tracts remained undeveloped until the middle of the 19th Century.[3] The principle reason that the land remained unsettled for a number of years was that the Comanche, a hostile tribe, made war on the Apaches and settlers alike. The Comanche at the time claimed all lands in that particular area.

The Comanche continued to be a problem for early settlers in the Texas Hill Country until 1845 when a German immigrant named John O. Meusebach was named the commissioner of the Society for the Protection of German Immigrants in Texas. In this position, Meusebach was charged with overseeing the care of some 5,000 immigrants who depended upon the Society for their daily needs. These people were in a pioneer land where scarcities were made more acute because of the war between the United States and Mexico in 1845.[4]

For the protection of the settlement and its new Texas citizens, Meusebach determined to go into the vast Fisher-Miller tract to attempt to make a peace treaty with the Comanche. This was a very hazardous undertaking so the governor of Texas sent Major Robert S. Neighbors to stop Meusebach because of the danger. However, the determined commissioner was far into Comanche country before the soldier-Indian agent joined the group in what is now Mason County near the present-day community of Katemcy located on FM 1222 just east of Camp Air on U.S. Highway 87.[5]

The Comanche chief Ketemoczy agreed to bring the other tribal chiefs to a designated meeting place on the San Saba

River at the next full moon. The German group, made up of surveyors, helpers and guides, returned to Fredericksburg. At the appointed time, Meusebach and Neighbors returned with a smaller group of men carrying various gifts and trade goods. The meeting was held about where Brady Creek flows into the San Saba River. A Texas State Historical Marker is located near the meeting site on present day FM 2732 some eight miles southwest of Harkeyville.[6]

The treaty that was signed by some 20 chiefs and sub-chiefs came about after several days of negotiations, trading and feasting. The Indians took a fancy to Meusebach, fascinated by his red beard. They called him "El Sol Colorado."[7] As a result of the treaty, an additional thousands of acres of Fisher-Miller Grant land was opened up to newly arriving colonists and gave them a measure of protection from future Indian depredations.[8] Although there were occasional Indian raids seeking horses, mules and cattle, few settlers in the German settlements were killed or kidnapped after the treaty was signed.

---

[1] The Lackey Tragedy in Blanco County first appeared in the <u>Blanco News</u> and was later re-printed in the <u>Frontier Times Magazine</u>, Bandera, Texas, April 1936. It was republished in the <u>Blanco County History</u>, Burnet Texas, Nortex, 1979, by John Stribling Moursund, pages 414-416, copy provided by the Texas Collection, Baylor University, Waco, Texas.

[2] "Blanco County," <u>The Handbook of Texas Online</u>, <http://www.tshaonline.org/handbook/online/>

[3] Ibid.

[4] Gillespie County Historical Society, <u>Pioneers in God's Hills, A History of Fredericksburg and Gillespie County, People and Events</u>, (Austin, TX: Eakin Publications, 1983).

[5] <u>The Texas Almanac Sesquicentennial Edition,1857-2007</u>.

[6] Ibid.

[7] Gillespie County Historical Society, op. cit.

[8] Ibid.

Chapter 13:
Did A Mob Kill A Child?

For more than a Century, Babyhead Mountain situated about nine and half miles north of Llano, has been a mystery. The so-called mountain, actually more like a rugged brush covered hill, was the site of one of the most gruesome killings ever to happen in Llano County.

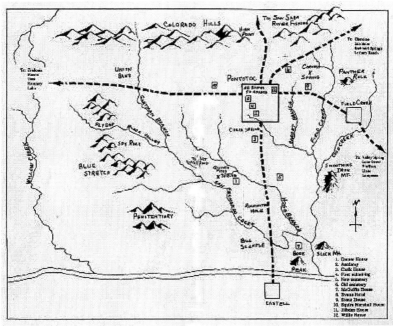

Map of the area where much rustling was carried out by mobs. The once prosperous community of Pontotoc was a trading center for many years, and included an academy for young adults. Map from the Ross McSwain collection.

Tragically, the dismembered body of a missing child, her head severed from her tiny body and impelled on a stick near the hilltop, gave the place its controversial name.

For years people living in the vicinity of the hill speculated that the vicious murder of the child was another barbarous crime blamed on hostile Comanche or Kiowa Indians and the child's head was left as a warning to Anglos moving into the area that they were tracking into forbidden hunting grounds.

Who was the little girl? Who were the parents? Where did they live? Who discovered the child's body, and where was she buried? None of these questions were ever fully answered, but over the years stories surfaced that shed some light on the mystery. In fact, some of the answers "muddled the water" some more, resulting in added speculation of a conspiracy.

The late John Edwin Conner, teacher, college dean and professor of history for some 25 years at Texas A&M University – Kingsville, formerly called South Texas State Teachers College and later Texas A&I, was born in Llano County in 1883. He lived for a number of years in the Pontotoc-Field Creek area where his father, William T. Conner, farmed and operated a general store. His mother, Harriet, was postmistress at Pontotoc.

After graduating from school in 1904, Conner started teaching in one-room schools, including serving the communities of Katemcy and Fredonia. Later he would teach in a number of West Texas schools, including Eden, Eldorado, Odessa, Sanderson and Alpine before taking a teaching position at the Kingsville school. While attending school at Pontotoc, he was influenced by the late E. C. Broyles, who got Conner interested in studying history and taught him how to write clearly and persuasively. Broyles was the great-grandfather of William Broyles, who later was editor of *Texas Monthly* magazine.[1]

In 1983, when Conner was in his 90s, his daughter-in-law, Katherine Conner, put some of Conner's reminiscences together into a book titled *A Great While Ago*. In the book,

Conner wrote about the Babyhead Mountain killing, repeating things he heard as a child, including stories about Indian raids, murders, rustlers, horse thieves and activities of the mobs. According to Conner, these things were just subjects of conversations in those days.

"The Indians who were in the Packsaddle Mountain battle were sometimes held responsible for the death of Bill Buster's daughter," Conner related. The Buster cabin was located where Pecan Creek flowed into the Llano River, and the child had been captured. A few days later the child's decapitated body was found on the mountain then called the Colorado Hills.[2]

Conner also relates that the date of the child's death was in August 1873, and that she was named Mary Elizabeth. For many years there was a question about the year of the death or of the child's identity. Although there remain conflicts concerning the death, a few years ago a Llano man told writer Dale Fry that an uncle had told him that his father revealed that a "local mob of powerful and wealthy ranchers" killed the little girl and had blamed it on the Indians.[3]

"When I was 14, my Uncle David Webster told me that his father, M. L. Webster, told him that a local mob killed the little girl. They came to M.L.'s father, Nathaniel Webster, and told him they were going to massacre a whole family of homesteaders. They gave him three reasons why and asked him to participate in it," said Ned Cook.[4]

According to Cook, the reasons for killing the family were that they were "poor white trash," there had been frequent Indians raids, and the ranchers and homesteaders alike wanted the U.S. Cavalry to dispatch a unit to the area for protection, and they (the ranchers) wanted to discourage more settlers from coming in and staking claims on their lands. "My great-grandfather Webster was an honorable man and told them he wanted no part of it," Cook said.[5]

According to Fry's story, no one ever suspected the "mob of reputable citizens" because they quickly spread the rumor that the Indians had killed the child.[6]

"If this version is true – the only objective they achieved was to come out free of blame for the crime," writes Fry. "This startling version could also explain why those who had knowledge of the details were so close-mouthed about them. Fear of the mob was more than enough to guarantee the silence of even the most notorious gossipers."[7]

Conner recalled that his "Uncle Jim" was a cowboy during those days when lots of cattle were being run in the Mason-San Saba-Llano-McCulloch County area. The biggest ranchers were the Lathams, but the uncle also worked for the Littlefield and White outfit. The Lathams were, by far, the largest operators with herds in several counties stretching from Burnet County to the San Angelo country. The Latham headquarters was located in the southwest corner of San Saba County.[8]

"Cattle rustlers had to be watched for and reported," Conner observed. Deputy Sheriff Thomas Henry Nowlin was killed in the Pontotoc area when he went to serve papers on a rustler who had been indicted on a charge of burning a brand. The warrant for the man's arrest was from Jeff Davis County, in far West Texas.

There were horse thieves, too. One of the methods in that racket was well organized. For instance, a man would steal a horse in Pontotoc just after dark, ride him to Fredonia, ten miles away, there to meet a man who had stolen a horse at Katemcy, ten miles further west. The two would exchange horses at Fredonia and ride home and be seen at home or riding around town the next morning.

The next night the Pontotoc man would ride the Katemcy horse to Valley Springs, ten miles to the east, and there meet another man with a horse stolen in Lone Grove, ten miles east of Valley Springs. Thus a stolen horse could be one hundred miles away within a week, and none of the thieves would have been away from home during the time,"[9] Conner explained.

The only way a man could be caught was if he was seen riding too many different horses about town.

The shooting of Deputy Nowlin was also a sad affair. He had been serving as a Llano County lawman for only a month before his untimely death on April 5, 1888.

Kimble County historian Frederica Wyatt of Junction provided the following information on Nowlin's death. The shooting happened this way, according to court records in Austin:

Nowlin was given the warrant to arrest a man named Jim Jones by Llano County Sheriff Caldwell Roberts. Nowlin and Jones were acquainted and lived within two miles of each other, so what happened later was unexpected.

Nowlin, accompanied by a Llano County citizen named Lee Peck, went to Jones' home located in neighboring San Saba County less than a mile from the Llano County line. Peck would later testify before a coroner's hearing that when Nowlin was about thirty feet from Jones' residence, he called out for Jones to come out. Jones responded, saying he would be out "in a minute." When he came out the front door, he was carrying a double barrel shotgun.

Nowlin told Jones he had a court paper for him. Jones said he thought the visitors were perhaps members of a mob "as some around here have been accusing me of stealing horses." During this conversation, Peck said he and the deputy dismounted from their horses and walked up to the door where Jones was standing. When Jones asked for the paper, Nowlin gave him the warrant explaining that it was from Jeff Davis County. Jones asked Nowlin to explain some of the wording on the paper. When he did so, Jones raised his shotgun and fired both barrels at the same time.

Unknown to Jones, Nowlin had drawn his pistol while the man was reading the paper. They fired at each other virtually at the same time. Nowlin staggered about 15 to 20 feet from the door and fell, but fired a shot at Jones a second time as his body hit the ground.

Peck told the coroner that he quickly left the area and went for help. He returned with a Doctor Anderson about two hours before Nowlin died. Peck told the court that when he returned with the doctor that the mortally wounded Nowlin had been moved inside the Jones home.

Dr. R. B. Anderson testified that Deputy Nowlin was shot in the back, four or five inches above the base of the spinal column, some of the shot passing through the front of the body, and other shot lodging in front of the right hip. The doctor said he talked to the wounded lawman about his wound and the shooting scrape. Nowlin died about two hours later.

Jim Jones was arrested later and charged with Nowlin's death. He was found guilty of second-degree murder in a San Saba County court and given a sentence of 24 years in the state penitentiary. He appealed the case, however, and it was reversed and remanded by the Appeals Court.[10]

In a series of stories on the settling of the Texas Hill Country and the Hoo-Doo War that was waged in Mason County in 1874-1876, Peter R. Rose of Austin, historian and geologist noted that in the years 1870-1880, Burnet, Lampasas, Llano, Mason, McCulloch, Kimble, Kerr, San Saba, Gillespie and Blanco counties were open rangeland. He stated that the most common industry in that region was gathering wild cattle, principally Longhorns, by local ranchers and their neighbors. These cattle were to supply the livestock for businessmen filling beef contracts so the herds were trailed northward to Kansas railheads for markets in the industrialized eastern United States.[11]

As a result of all these loose cattle roaming all over Southern Texas, Confederate Army veterans, along with deserters, jayhawkers and others soon were working the brush country gathering unbranded animals and either selling them or establishing ranches. Those settlers that had arrived in the area before the war did not freely relinquish land or cattle to these newcomers. Violence soon followed.

"As the Indian danger diminished in the 1870s, the Edwards Plateau area began to harbor outlaws, especially in those locations which previously had been most vulnerable to Indian attacks," said Rose. "Desperados were attracted to such areas by the sparseness of permanent residents, the absence of organized county governments and the law, and the abundant hiding places provided by the dark, well watered coves and hollows around the Plateau…and lawmen did not venture into the region."[12]

According to Rose, many Hill Country communities were long delayed in being officially organized and "law-abiding." In fact, different ethnic groups, such as the German immigrants and the Anglo settlers, "behaved tribally," and found themselves on opposite sides of the law. As a result, vigilante groups sprang up when generally law-abiding citizens lost patience and faith with legal authorities. Soon these groups were abusing the very law they professed to uphold.[13]

In some cases, Rose reports, groups of outlaws actually outnumbered the lawful citizens and at times took over control of county governments through intimidation and collusion. In many of the counties, such as Llano, Burnet, Lampasas, Mason, Menard and Kimble, law-abiding government was established only after Texas Rangers intervened. Violence erupted even in Gillespie County, where German immigrants first settled in 1846.

The German immigrants were mostly farmers, says Rose. "They came, not as new Texans, but as new Americans." They came for land and to escape military conscription and the continuous political unrest that was brought about by early attempts to unify Germany.[14]

Ironically, the peace-loving German settlers also faced mob violence. In 1846, when the German colonists were getting settled in New Braunfels, waiting to be led to their acreage toward present-day Fredericksburg, a man named

Phillip Cappes capitalized on the unrest and unhappiness of the colonists to set up a plot to help stage a revolt against the settlers' Commissioner-General. A mob formed and the angry group, led by a "disgruntled Rudolph Iwonski," started making a list of demands, including that leader-business manager John O. Meusebach resign.[15]

Despite the shouts of "hang him," the threat of a whipping and other indignities, Meusebach remained unruffled; he stood quietly and talked to the mob in measured tones. Presently, the mob of about 120 men started to disperse, not before a full box of cigars had been handed out to the men.

On the afternoon of the mob's misbehavior, a group of Americans living in New Braunfels came to Meusebach to express their indignation over the event and stated their willingness to stand by him "to their last drop of blood." On the following day – January 1, 1847 – a group of Americans and German colonists assembled and passed resolutions condemning the action of the mob and declared it a slander to the wishes of the community.[16]

Things calmed down in the German settlements until the Civil War broke out and Texans were faced with having to decide whether to vote for secession from the Union and join the Confederacy. When the vote came, a majority of the German colonists were loyal to the Union. When the Confederacy attempted to conscript the Germans in 1862 for service in the Confederate Army, a group of some sixty men from the Fredericksburg-Comfort area attempted to go to Mexico and either live their until hostilities were over or attempt to join Union forces. While camped near the Nueces River on the night of July 2, 1862, they were surprised by some 100 Confederate militia. After a brutal battle that lasted several hours, a large number of Germans were killed and others seriously wounded. Those were later executed. Germans who escaped were later tracked to the Rio Grande where they, too, were shot down.[17]

When the German settlers in the Fredericksburg area recognized that war was inevitable, a volunteer force was organized under the command of Captain Frank van der Stucken to protect the settlements from Indians who were more likely to commit raids when they knew that men folk were away.

In her book relating the frontier life of her father, John Meusebach, Irene Marschall King notes that as the situation gradually showed improvement, the young Germans residing west of Fredericksburg – in the Doss, Cherry Springs, Loyal Valley communities – were regarded as "Unionists." The Americans residing in the area, almost all Southern sympathizers resented them. As a result, some individuals took matters into their own hands without regard to laws or justice. According to King, an example of this happened to four young German farmers who, on the basis of false charges, were forced from their homes. The next morning the four were found hanging on trees not far from their houses.[18]

Even among the usual placid German immigrants, mob violence was a common occurrence. Mob law was enforced by a bunch of renegades known as the "Hanging Band." The immigrants reacted in several different ways to the various outranges committed by the group, including hiding near their homes, staying silent and not talking about the gang. The Germans called the mob the "bushwhackers." Those that stayed home and away from the war and secretly supported the Union paid a dear price for their convictions. "Many were distrusted and the renegades often inflicted atrocities," King wrote.[19]

According to King, much of the injustice could be traced to certain individuals not native to the area. Under the cloak of patriotism, she said, mob violence once started swept like a prairie fire. With the close of the Civil War, the causes of friction among the settlers and their neighbors were removed and gradually peace was restored to the communities.

However, some animosity continued for another generation.

[1] "Conner, John Edwin," The Handbook of Texas Online, <http://www.tshaonline.org/handbook/online/>

[2] John E. Conner, A Great While Ago, (Austin, TX: Eakin Publications Inc., 1983).

[3] Dale Fry. "Babyhead Mountain Mystery," The Texas Heartland Website.

[4] Ibid.

[5] Ibid.

[6] Ibid.

[7] Ibid.

[8] Conner, op. cit.

[9] Ibid.

[10] Frederica Wyatt, Junction, E-mail communication to author, June 14, 2004.

[11] Peter R. Rose, presentation at Mason County Historical Commission's seminar on the Hoo-Doo War, Mason, TX, May 5, 2002.

[12] Ibid.

[13] Ibid.

[14] Ibid.

[15] Irene Marschall King, John O. Meusebach, German Colonizer in Texas, (Austin, TX: University of Texas Press, 1967) p. 102-103.

[16] Ibid. p. 103.

[17] Ibid., p. 158.

[18] Ibid., p. 159.

[19] Ibid., p. 159.

Chapter 14:
Tarnished Badges

On occasion he wore a deputy sheriff's badge. He also had the reputation of being one of the old west's most ruthless gunmen. Texas after the Civil War and the end of Reconstruction was not a place for the shy or the timid. Jim Miller was not shy or timid, but he was known to have the best manners among those frontier pistoleros.

A native of Van Buren, Arkansas, Miller came into the Texas heartland as an infant when his parents moved to Franklin. When his mother and father died, he was sent to live with his grandparents at Langford's Cove, now Evant in Coryell County. When he was about eight years old, the elderly couple was murdered and the boy was arrested for the killing but never prosecuted.

He was then sent to live with his sister and her husband, a man named J. E. Coop, on their farm at Plum Creek, a small settlement near Gatesville. Young Jim never got along with his brother-in-law, who would become a victim of a gunshot after the pair had gotten into a violent argument. Although Miller, then 17, was charged with murder, tried and given a sentence of life imprisonment, the case, like many others that went to court in those days, was overturned on appeal and he was never retried.[1]

Jim Miller was nothing like the prototype old west gunslinger. He was an immaculate dresser, favoring crisp white shirts, long coat, and well-tailored trousers. He was usually well groomed; thick moustache trimmed and clean-shaved face. Some people called him "Deacon Jim" because he was a regular at church services and was well versed in the Bible.

But old west historian Leon Metz says folks knew him as "Killing Jim," a cold-blooded, almost inhuman individual who raised the art of bushwhacking and ambush to an exact science.[2] His weapon of choice was a shotgun hidden beneath his long coat, and he sometimes wore a makeshift bulletproof vest of boilerplate. It saved his life on several occasions.

Miller found his way into the Texas heartland when he married Sally Clements, the daughter of McCulloch County rancher-trail driver Manning "Mannie" Clements Sr. and a cousin of the notorious John Wesley Hardin, perhaps the most deadly gunman in the Southwest.

Like many early settlers in Central Texas, Miller got into the cattle business with his father-in-law and made numerous visits to Brady City and to its neighboring communities of Richland Springs and San Saba. During one of his forays into San Saba he crossed paths with then Deputy Sheriff Dee Harkey, brother of Sheriff Joe Harkey, who had a warrant for Miller's arrest for some minor offense. Rather than dispute the charge, Miller paid a modest fine and went on about his business.

Harkey, though young in years, had already escaped being fatally shot by a girlfriend who was protecting her father from being arrested for stock theft. He was no stranger to violence and would not back down if confronted.

According to historian Bill O'Neal, Miller drifted around Central Texas and the Mexican border country and operated a saloon in San Saba for a period of time before ending up just west of the Pecos River wearing a badge as a Reeves County deputy sheriff.

"While in Pecos, Miller became involved in a feud with Sheriff G. A. "Bud" Frazer, who accused Miller of stealing a pair of mules. The two men exchanged gunshots with one another in a Pecos street but each suffered only minor injuries. Later, however, Miller found Frazer in a Toyah saloon and blasted him to eternity. Again, Miller was acquitted of the murder on grounds that "he had done no worse than Frazer."[3]

The Miller-Clements family connection was very close.

Emmanuel "Mannen" Clements and his brothers, Gyp, Jim and Joe, were reared on a cattle ranch south of Smiley, a community located east of Nixon in Gonzales County.

The Clements brothers and friends. Seated in center is Joe Clements. Seated at right is believed to be Mannen Clements Sr. Figure standing second from left is believed to be Jim Clements. Others are unidentified. These men were well known in the Texas Heartland and each had a tough reputation. Photo from the Robert J. Mullin Collection, J. Evetts Haley Library, Midland.

Their cousin, John Wesley Hardin, seeking a hideout after getting into trouble, came to stay on the Clements ranch in 1871. When the Clements brothers took a herd of cattle up the trail to Kansas, Hardin went along as a cowhand. According to historian O'Neal, Hardin later helped the Clements family when they got involved in the Taylor-Sutton feud. Mannen and his brothers, Jim, Joe and Gyp, were involved in the dispute on the Taylor side. The Clements' and the Taylors were related.[4]

Emanuel "Mannen" Clements Sr., Central Texas rancher and brother of Jim, Joe and Gip Clements, cousins of the notorious John Wesley Hardin. Mannen also was the father-in-law of Deacon Jim Miller. Photo courtesy Division of Manuscripts, University of Oklahoma Libraries.

Mannen Clements was a well-known rancher in McCulloch and San Saba counties where he had accumulated vast horse and cattle herds. He also had more than a nodding acquaintance with several of his cousin's running mates, including Bill Taylor, John Ringo and several members of the Sam Bass gang who he met while being held in the Austin jail.[5]

The late J. E. Shropshire, who was a young man in his late twenties when he arrived in Brady City in April 1893 to open his law practice, remembered the Clements family well when he published portions of his memoirs in the *McCulloch County News* on April 28, 1944. Shropshire recalled that the Clements were involved in the Taylor-Sutton feud that had taken place a number of years earlier, and that "when the thing was finally broken up, many of the Taylors had moved into this section (McCulloch County) of the state. The notorious John Wesley Hardin was a member of the Taylor branch of the feud, and those people, in the main, lived desperate lives to their deaths.[6]

"There was a man by the name of Jim Clements who lived near Brady when I first came to this county. Jim Clements was a first cousin of John Wesley Hardin, and he and his brother, Mannen Clements, lived in this vicinity, and relatives of theirs by the name of Miller lived in and around here at one time. They were all bold and desperate men who had been reared in this feud in Southwest Texas," Shropshire wrote.[7]

According to Shropshire, Jim Clements was ranching in the area with his brother and was handling principally horses. A short time after he had opened his small law office on the south side of the courthouse in Brady, a woman came into his office. She was crying and told the young lawyer that her husband had left her and had taken her baby boy and would not allow her to see the child. She wanted to know what could be done about it. Shropshire did not know the woman's name.

Having little courtroom experience at that time, Shropshire had to refer to his law books. He told the woman he could not do anything as long as she remained the wife of her husband, and the only remedy he knew of was for her to get a divorce and have the District Court give custody of the child to her.

After discussing the cost of such court action – $50 – the still unidentified woman said she would have to get financial help from her brother. During the interview, the woman showed Shropshire a deep scar on her face that was the result of a fight she had with the husband, and she asked the attorney to write her brother and explain the situation.

"I learned who she was when I went to take down the information needed for the petition to the court," Shropshire wrote.[8]

"Then I realized for the first time that I had to deal with so desperate a man." In a few days, the woman returned to Shropshire's office, crying again, and said she was fearful that her husband would do personal violence to her and she wanted to know how to protect herself. He advised her she needed to see the justice of the peace and have him placed under a peace bond. A requirement for putting Jim Clements under a peace bond was to have him arrested and brought before the JP for a hearing on the matter.

Apparently Jim Clements' reputation was widespread. When the warrant was issued, local officers were reluctant to serve it because they feared the man.

"Finally, a young fellow in the community named Andy Locklear said he would serve the warrant if he was deputized.[9] Locklear, the new deputy, brought Clements to the courthouse where he was placed under a $1,000 bond. The rancher promptly made bond and left.

As a result of Clements' arrest and being placed under a peace bond, matters seemed to attract a great amount of attention in the community, Shropshire noted in his memoirs.

"It seemed to me that Jim Clements was the most feared man in all this community; in fact it seemed that the officers as well as everyone else feared him," Shropshire recalled. For weeks, or perhaps a month after filing the suit for divorce, a deputy came to Shropshire's office one morning to warn him that Clements was in town carrying a Winchester "with its magazine full of cartridges and furiously mad at me and swearing all kinds of vengeance because of my having filed the suit against him."[10]

The deputy advised Shropshire to just send word to Clements that he would drop the suit and have nothing else to do with it because, "he is mad and will kill you. At that remark, I looked out in front of my office and saw Clements sitting on the steps leading over the high fence of courthouse with his Winchester in his hand apparently waiting for my reply to this warning," Shropshire recalled.[11]

Shropshire refused to be intimidated, and told the deputy to get Sheriff Jim Wall to disarm the man. Wall did so. During the lull, Shropshire slipped out the back door and went home to fetch a six-shooter that he placed on top of his desk.

An hour or so later, Sheriff Wall went to Shropshire's office and asked him if he would be willing to talk to Clements. The young lawyer agreed to meet the man, but told the sheriff to have Clements leave the Winchester outside. According to Shropshire's memoir, Clements appeared never to understand that the matter was strictly a civil court action, but the man left the office without further threats.

"The matter rested again for a number of weeks until one day three men came into my office. They were armed to the teeth. One of them introduced himself as Mrs. Clements brother and the others as relatives of hers. They told me they had come in response to the letter I had written for her, appealing for aid. They wanted to know where they could find Jim Clements, and then whether it would be best to go out and see him or have him come in to talk with them. They decided to send word to have him come to town."[12]

The men and Clements met in front of the hotel. Each presented their arms to show it was a peaceful meeting, Shropshire related. After the gathering, the trio returned to the law office and said the matter had been settled. The suit for divorce would be dropped and Mrs. Clements would go home with the brother and other relatives. Anxious to be rid of Clements and his threats, Shropshire said his charge for getting the suit dismissed would be a nominal $10.

"Well, I dismissed the suit and she went home with her brother and relatives. The brother said to me that when she went down there to visit, it would be a very prolonged visit; that is, that she would not return, and that if Jim Clements ever came down there it would be just too bad for him. It seemed that Jim Clements and his wife had married across that deadly feud line between the Taylors and the Suttons," Shropshire said. [13]

Although nothing serious ever happened, Jim Clements continued to be a threat to Shropshire for months to come, riding by his office with a Winchester across his lap, or eyeing him with brutal, mean looks whenever he was in Brady City.

After a lapse of considerable time, Clements disappeared from the county, and not long afterward Shropshire read in a San Antonio newspaper where the same three men who had visited him to settle the matter were being held in jail there, apparently on murder charges, but were later released when the state was unable to produce a body. Shropshire never revealed the identity of the men in his memoirs.

"It was later reported that they (lawmen investigators) had found Jim Clements' saddle in a cave, but they never had found Jim Clements' body, dead or alive," Shropshire noted. "That was the only time in my life that I ever felt relief that a man was dead. I have never, from a reliable source, heard of or from Jim Clements since."[14]

As Shropshire notes in his unpublished memoirs, victims of feuds and mob violence were routinely never found, thus many cases were marked closed.

While living in Brownwood before locating his law office in Brady, Shropshire recalled attending a trial in District Court in which the confessed facts "were the most disgusting, I believe, of any I have ever heard before or since. A man living out there toward the boundary of Mills County had come into the Brown County District Court, gone before the grand jury and accused his neighbor of the most infamous crime that I had ever heard presented by an indictment – or heard of.

"The accused man indignantly denied the charge, demand a trial, and was acquitted. The evidence showed that the prosecuting witness had maliciously perjured himself to slander his neighbor. The grand jury then returned an indictment against the falsifying witness for perjury. Imagine his defense. He admitted the perjury, but said he had to do so for fear of his life because the Mills County Mob had ordered him to do so."[15]

Shropshire observed that had he been in that man's place, "the mob would have gotten me before I succumbed to such threats.

"That infamous Mills County Mob sent its tentacles into Brown County, thence over the river into San Saba County, and was penetrating McCulloch County when I moved here (to Brady)," Shropshire observed.[16] "Men were being ambushed and murdered all around until the Rangers moved in on it at San Saba and dispersed the thing. Those feuds and mobs of former years had the habit, sometimes, of a prairie fire that sweeps the whole countryside."

---

[1] Leon Claire Metz, The Shooters, (New York, NY: Berkley Books, 1996) p. 155.

[2] Ibid., p. 155.

[3] Bill O'Neal, Encyclopedia of Western Gunfighters, (Norman, OK: University of Oklahoma Press, 1979) p. 231.

[4] Ibid., p. 64.

[5] Ibid., p. 65.

[6] Wayne Spiller, Handbook of McCulloch County History, Volume II, (Brady, TX: Staked Plains Press, 1976) p. 5.

[7] Ibid., p. 6.

[8] Ibid., p. 6.

[9] Ibid., p. 6.

[10] Ibid., p. 7.

[11] Ibid., p. 7.

[12] Ibid., p. 7.

[13] Ibid., p. 8.

[14] Ibid., p. 8.

[15] Ibid., p. 9.

[16] Ibid., p. 9.

Chapter 15:
Reflections On Mob Activities

Mob activities that gripped much of the Texas heartland during the years immediately following the Civil War were oftentimes the topic of everyday conversation but mostly were limited to only talks with close friends or acquaintances – persons that could be trusted. Folks living and working in those counties were concerned for their welfare and for their personal safety and expressed those fears.

Since beginning research about this violent period of time in Texas history, more and more stories have surfaced from various sources; some from recollections made during long-ago interviews conducted by unemployed writers working in the Federal Writers Project, 1936-1940.

Responding to a crippling depression, the federal government, endorsed by President Franklin D. Roosevelt, adopted an activist role in the economy and society. The New Deal, as Roosevelt called his plan, was pushed forward to resolve the crisis of a collapsing financial system, a crippling unemployment rate, and breakdowns in agriculture and industry that were causing national anxiety.

Within this complex New Deal program was a relief agency known as the Works Progress Administration (WPA), which was set up to assist the unemployed and boost the economy. Before it ended in 1943, the WPA had given jobs to 9 million people and had spent nearly $12 billion. While most of these jobs and funds went into public building projects, such as schools, post offices, hospitals, parks and roads, it also developed projects for unemployed writers, musicians and actors.

In response, the American Guide Series of the Federal Writers' Project was established. It would become one of the

132

most ambitious research and writing undertakings in American history. The project would put writers to work preparing state guidebooks, writing historical pamphlets, interviewing pioneers and recording points of interest. Various work districts were set up in each state that chose to participate in the program. Texas was one among those that took part in the writing project.

The information gathered in interviews conducted with former cowboys, ranch operators, business leaders and even former slaves was tucked away in federal files for many years and was not widely circulated or published. Today, however, many of these interviews can be found on the internet.

James E. Shultz was 74 years old when he talked with writer Sheldon Gauthier in Fort Worth in 1939. He was born in 1865 on a farm at Falls Creek in Llano County. As a young man he worked as a cowboy during roundups, and later as a regular cowhand on the sprawling Duncan Ranch, one of the largest at that time in the Texas Hill Country. He was among the witnesses to a gun battle that raged between two factions of cattlemen in the streets of Llano.

"There were some right pert ranches in that section, and many small grease-pot outfits. The Duncan outfit was about the largest ranch in the county, with the Pullum, Harmon and John Burns ranches running up in fair-sized outfits," Shultz said.[1]

The retired farmer-rancher rag rug factory worker recalled his many years as a working cowboy participating in roundups with other ranch cowboys. "The cow outfits in that section worked together in a general way, doing about all the range work. There were riders from each outfit looking after the herds, looking for sick and injured animals, and keeping cattle from straying too far," he said. This was the time of open range.

"There were two things that kept the ranchers with their weathered eye peeled; that was for rustlers stealing cattle and Indians stealing horses and committing other depredations," he

133

said.[2]

"The rustler trouble reached a point in that section at one time when it was not safe for folks to talk about either side of the question. There was an organization of two factions – the 'pures' and 'rustlers.' The condition was so tense that one had to keep his trap closed or get branded, or be banned from the county. If a party received notice to leave the country, from either side, such party had to leave the country pronto, within the time limit, or be willing to have his hide punctured and his friends put to the trouble of digging a little hole for him. The territory included Llano and Mills counties. In this section there were several people who were members of one or the other faction, who left the country hurriedly, and some who were not members. Some folks stayed after getting a notice to leave, but were taken out of circulation as a reward for staying."[3]

In the interview, Shultz recalled talking to a young schoolteacher who had come to Llano to teach. The men had met in the local wagon yard, and there were other persons standing around hearing their conversation.

"During our talk, he (Reed) gave his mind about the killings and said it ought to be stopped. The following Monday morning he was walking on a path going to the school and came to a piece of paper tied to a string, hanging on a pole that had been placed overhead across the path. On the paper was written this message: 'Keep your trap shut.' He replaced the paper after writing a reply, 'I am a stranger here and need advice. Thanks.' After that incident the teacher refused to talk about anything, except the weather, and was careful what he said about that."

In another instance, Shultz told about another man who told a bunch of people at the wagon yard that he could put his hands on the parties who were mixed up in a certain killing.

"Within a week after that talk, while riding to where his son was fixing a cattle pen and when within 100 yards of the pen, his son heard a gunshot; looking up, he saw his father falling out of the saddle. The boy ran to his father and found him dead, with a bullet hole in his head," Shultz recalled.[4]

The former Llano County cowboy also said he witnessed a real battle between several members of a rustler faction one day in Llano. He said a man named John Hartley was the head of one side and John Merit was head of the other side.

"Most of the parties were related by marriage and had been working together. It seemed that some of the men were accused by the others of snitching," Shultz said. "I was standing in front of the Jim Phillips' Saloon talking with Jim and he was telling me that he expected to see some excitement because there was a crowd of some 25 men gunning for each other, and that if it got started hell would be popping. Just about the time he finished talking we heard shots that sounded like a bunch of firecrackers exploding, and the fight was on.

In the next block from the saloon, one bunch was barricaded in an old shack. The others were on the outside, attacking and shooting from behind cover. Hartley's nephew started to run from behind a tree to get closer to the shack but was killed by a bullet out of his uncle's gun. Hartley was shot at and hit three times while standing in the door making his shot at the boy," Shultz noted.[5] "That fight sort of cooled off the killings, and from that time on things became more orderly."

Shultz said he worked for the Duncan Ranch until he quit ranch work in 1900 and started farming. He married and moved into a house rather than living in a range camp. He was living in Fort Worth at the time of the interview. He had worked for several years in a rag rug factory until June 1938 when he quit "because my eyes were not equal to the work."

J. A. Joiner of San Angelo, Texas, was born in 1855 in Mississippi and came to Burnet County in February 1870. He was interviewed on March 23-28, 1938, at his home on East 18th Street by Ruby Mosley when he was 85 years old.

"Llano and San Saba counties had their share of outlaws and underworld characters. The rough element was feared by the little German settlement (Castell) in Llano County. They decided among themselves that they needed protecting. They planned a little trap that caught one of the most dreaded crooks, Mose Beard. They were glad to put that rough character under earth," Joiner recalled. "John Beard, a brother of Mose, had been running wild with him and felt it his duty to get his man. There was about twelve in the little gang that killed Mose. John went in there and killed most of them and skipped out. The friends and enemies left behind later heard that John was killed at a Fandango in Old Mexico. Later I met up with a friend that had visited John and said he was a successful rancher in old Mexico. Scott Cooley, George Gladden and John Ringo were killers but I never knew their outcome. There were many more outlaws of that section that I cannot safely mention," Joiner said.[6] Like many others, Joiner was still reluctant to talk about mob days and those involved even after the passage of more than fifty years.

Mrs. Robert Lindsey, 59, of Fort Worth, told interviewer Woody Phipps in 1940 that she grew up on her grandfather's ranch in San Saba County. While living with her grandfather and helping to keep house on the ranch, she recalled that a mob of large ranchers sought to control the county and force others to leave. "This reign of terror went on for a number of years," she said. It (the mob) was still active after she married Robert Lindsey, a cowboy, and left the county to live with him near Brownwood.[7]

Mrs. Lindsey recalled that her grandfather's ranch was not very large, but was "one of the best grassed and watered places around that part of the country. That made it valuable and several ranchers were always deviling grandfather to sell out. He wouldn't do it because that was his home.

That was one of the reasons a bunch of men bunched up and tried to run other ranchers out of the county. They called the gang The Mob. It was always hard for me to understand just why they would do the things they did. They killed Shorty Brown, my grandmother's brother, after they told him to leave and he wouldn't. The whole county turned out to hunt for him when he come up missing, and they found him hung to a tree in his pasture by the creek. His son inherited the ranch and they sent him notices to leave, but he wouldn't leave either. I saw those men ride by lots of times," she said.[8]

According to Mrs. Lindsey's recollections, the riders never wore masks, and she recognized several of them. "They were big ranchers, prominent men in the county. That was why I could never understand because the men were so prominent, and yet be so mean. Two different sheriffs, one by the name of Hawkins, and the other Atkinson, were the leaders of the Mob."[9]

Mrs. Lindsey said her grandfather was sent notice after notice, but he did not bluff. "I saw several of the notices, and they had a crude scaffold drawn on them.

"One day, when all the family was going home from church, a shot just missed Shorty Brown's son. That was how bold they were, and once when my Daddy was in the hospital in Brownwood two men came in and chatted with him. After they left, he told me they were members of the Mob. He promised me that some day he would tell me the whole story about the Mob, but he died before he got to it," she said.[10]

Another old-timer that Woody Phipps talked to in 1940 was Ed Crawford, 68, who was born on his father's ranch in San Saba County in 1872. As a youth, Crawford worked for many different ranches, working cattle, breaking and training horses. He had to quit riding horses in 1913 when he broke his leg when a horse fell with him during the Fall Roundup. He sold his San Saba ranch in 1935 and was living there when he gave Phipps the writer's project interview. Crawford said he had two brothers, Bill Crawford, then living in Roswell, New Mexico, and Jack Crawford. Each spent most of their early youth working as cowboys on various ranches, he said.

For a time he worked for a man named Leon Blum, who had a horse ranch in Hill County. Crawford said he got his first experience in fence cutting while working on the Blum place.

"Blum was the first man in that part of the country to fence any size pasture. He fenced 4,000 acres, and it was every bit cut down in a week's time. You know, they didn't want no fences, and was ready to fight for open country. Blum didn't pay no never mind to them. He just went right on and fenced it right back. They never cut that one down, either," Crawford recalled.[11]

He remembered learning about the Mob operating in San Saba County while working on the Blum ranch.

"Nearly everybody's read about it in the newspapers, but they never got the full details, and I don't reckon no paper will ever be able to put it all together. It just takes somebody that has lived through it, like I done, and there's many a thing I'd never tell because I would not live to enjoy the fruits of such telling," he said. Crawford went on to explain how mob violence got started in Central Texas.

"There was a bunch of nesters and small cattlemen that did not have very good grass for their cattle, and they could not get any more land because other ranchers had already took it up. The only way those fellers could figure out to get more land was to scare these other ranchers plum out of the country, then take their land for a song.

"Now that sounds pretty good, but when they went to work scaring, they killed a man. Then, first thing you know, they killed another. When you have so many in a bunch your secret's bound to come out, so the ranchers found out about the scheme in short order. They couldn't get anything on the outlaw gang, so they started in fighting fire with fire."[12]

Crawford's description of how things progressed summed up what was happening during those fateful days of mob violence. Yet, the story is much more complex as a "murder society" develops which will keep a Central Texas county stirred up for nearly another decade.

[1] James E. Shultz, "American Life Histories, Manuscripts from the Federal Writers Project, 1936-1940, item No. 61, Texas Range Lore", American Memory from the Library of Congress Website, <http://lcweb2.loc.gov>.

[2] Ibid.

[3] Ibid.

[4] Ibid.

[5] Ibid.

[6] J.A. Joiner, "American Life Histories, manuscripts from the Federal Writers Project, 1936-1940, item No. 8, Texas Range Lore", American Memory from the Library of Congress Website, <http://lcweb2.loc.gov>.

[7] Mrs. Robert Lindsey, American Life Histories, manuscripts from the federal Writers Project, 1936-1940, item No. 1, Texas Range Lore", American Memory from the Library of Congress Website, <http://lcweb2.loc.gov>.

[8] Ibid.

[9] Ibid.

[10] Ibid.

[11] Ed Crawford, "American Life Histories, manuscript from the Federal Writers Project, 1936-1940, item No. 1, Texas Range Lore", American Memory from the Library of Congress Website, <http://lcweb2.loc.gov>.

[12] Ibid.

Chapter 16:
A Society Of Death

Beginning in about 1885 and continuing for the next 12 to 15 years, residents of San Saba County in the Texas heartland experienced some of the bleakest days of the century.

It was a time of mob rule when even respectable ranchers, farmers and businessmen were suspect. There was some speculation that several preachers held leadership roles in the mob. Law enforcement was poorly organized and several sheriffs also were suspected of mob involvement. No longer were settlers faced with late night raids by hostile Indians. Now the raiders wore hoods and behaved as bad or worse than any of the savages.

San Saba County, located in one of the most beautiful sections of Texas with sparkling, running waters, plentiful game and wildlife, rich soil and grass stirrup-high on a tall horse, had only a few sparsely populated settlements. Although the county was organized in 1856, it was months before any kind of local government started operation.

The town was still an infant community when the Civil War started in 1861. Secession and subsequent unrest kept things in turmoil until the war ended in 1865. It was then that battle-hardened Confederate soldiers started arriving into the area, seeking free land and livestock ready to be rounded up for sale to beef-hungry Yankees. These veterans of many bloody scrapes were quick to quarrel and to fight, each already had experience with various kinds of weaponry.

Along with the war veterans came gangs of horse thieves and cattle rustlers. There were incidences of fence cutting, allowing thieves to steal livestock. Regardless of the charges filed, not a single man was convicted by court juries during those early years.

To combat this lawlessness, a number of leading citizens, including seven prominent ranchers, several church leaders and others banded together and formed a secret organization of regulators, or vigilantes. The single purpose of the regulators, or mob, was to run the undesirables out of the county and those refusing to leave were caught and hanged or fatally shot.

According to folklore, family recollections and notes found in Texas Ranger reports, mob members would meet usually on a night of the full moon, gathering at a place called "Buzzards' Waterhole," located about eleven miles northwest of San Saba.

"This Society of Death was well organized," said Ranger Captain Bill McDonald. "It had an active membership of about 300, with obligations rigid and severe. Their meeting place was a small natural pool of water, almost surrounded by hills. It has the curiously appropriate name of 'Buzzards' Water Hole,' and here the worthy order of assassins assemble, once a month, usually during the full moon, to transact general business and to formulate plans for the removal of offending or superfluous friends."[1]

According to McDonald's report, later published in his biography, guards were posted during the meetings. Passwords were used among the members, as well as certain signs.

"They kept up the semblance of being inspired by lofty motives, and they maintained the forms that go with religious undertakings," said McDonald. "Being duly assembled to plot murder, they still opened their meetings with prayer."[2]

Several residents of the northwest area, then called the Post Oaks, recalled that they would occasionally encounter sentinels while riding by the water hole at night on their way home. A voice from the darkness would challenge them, saying "Go round. Go round." Persons hearing the warning would quickly take a detour.

The penalty for talking about the mob's activities was death, whether the talker was a member or not. As a result, it was nearly impossible to learn anything about them for years afterward; silence was the best defense against mob vengeance.

Texas Ranger Captain Bill McDonald, who broke the San Saba mob.
Photo courtesy Mike Cox collection, Austin, Texas.

"Even now, there is a memory in the blood of many an old Texan which makes him keep his lip firmly buttoned up when these matters are discussed," wrote historian C. L. Sonnichsen.[3]

A lot of people, many possibly innocent of any wrongdoing, died before the mobs were put out of business. When the Texas Rangers were called in to investigate and stop the violence in 1890, Sergeant W. J. L. Sullivan reported to his superiors that at one time the sheriffs of both San Saba and neighboring Mills County were either members of the mob or were controlled by the mob.

"Since 1880 San Saba has been the center of a disturbance, caused by the organization of a 'mob,' whose operations expanded into several other counties in that district," Sullivan recalled in his memoirs.

"A number of people had banded together to protect themselves against the depredations of cattle thieves and other criminals. The lawless element, of course, arrayed themselves against the mob faction. Many good people also lined up against it...Thus a strong organization called the 'anti-mob' grew in activity. The mob bunch, however, was the stronger...They elected one of their men as sheriff."[4]

Sullivan noted that the mob "did some good work" for a while, but like all organizations of that character, "it went too far and became more oppressive as it grew in power. Quite a number of bad citizens were slick enough to slip over to the stronger faction. They played a big part in changing the purpose of that organization from good to bad," he stated.[5] Lawlessness was encouraged on both sides, Sullivan added.

In an interview with W. A. Smith in San Saba on July 13, 1944, the late historian Charles Leland Sonnichsen, author of the book, *"I'll Die Before I Run,"* learned that while the outlaws were generally "poor specimens and desperados," they also were pretty smart. "It takes a smart man to be an outlaw, and they always have lots of friends," Smith said.[6]

"On the 'mob' side were deacons and even preachers. One preacher, though not active in the mob, had to stand up for his boys who were. There may have been some bad men among them, but mostly they were the best people," Smith continued.[7]

Smith told Sonnichsen that he and his family were not around after the first murder or two. It was the time of the great drought of 1885-1887. He and his father packed up the family and went over to Ellis County to pick cotton. They continued to hear rumors while living there.

"When the breakup (of the Mob) came, it was because a lot of citizens were convinced that the thing should be settled in the courtroom," Smith said in the interview. Smith told Sonnichsen that he never debated the matter with his close friends – who took the other side – even though he tended to agree with them.

Smith observed that the mob was known to have certain signs and passwords and would conduct "some sort of rituals" – more than likely on the order of Masonic rituals – things that local residents knew. He did not believe that the rituals came from the KGC – Knights of the Golden Circle – because the KGC "was never heard of in these parts."[8]

However, there were KGC chapters, or "castles," in a number of Texas localities, including LaGrange, Austin, San Antonio, Jefferson, Houston and Galveston. A number of prominent Texans were recruited as members, including then Gov. Sam Houston, but Houston was opposed to the KGC's anti-Union stand and refused to throw his support behind it.

The Knights of the Golden Circle, a secret order first recruited in the South, was formed in 1854 by a Cincinnati, Ohio, physician Dr. George W. L. Bickley, to support pro-slavery policies and promote the conquest of Mexico.[9]

During the Civil War, the organization was introduced into Indiana as an order of Peace Democrats or "Copperheads" to oppose Abraham Lincoln's war policy. The organization was connected with many acts of minor violence, but under the KGC name the order did not promote any serious plots against the Federal Government. In 1863, the group was reorganized as the Order of American Knights and later in 1864 was renamed the Sons of Liberty.

The KGC quietly dissolved during the Civil War. Some claimed that the organization operated as a fifth column in the North, and in the 1864 political campaign Republicans accused some anti-war Democrats of being secret members of the group. After the war, there were sporadic reports of KGC activities cropped up, some of them as far as West Texas and Oklahoma Territory, but by that time, for all intent and purposes, the organization had ceased to exist.[10]

B. J. Stubbs of Johnson City told Sonnichsen in an interview conducted on July 11, 1944, that a man named Bill Martin told the District Judge, a man named Allison, that he had a man who could clean things up by going up there (to San Saba County), get the confidence of the mob and provide evidence. He said Jim Shipp, a sharp lawyer, spent nearly an entire night talking with Sheriff A. J. Hawkins who told him who to see, what to say and what to look for.

The next morning, Shipp got on his horse and went back to Blanco. Martin saw him and wanted to know why he had come back so soon.

Martin said Shipp "god dammed him" and asked if he wanted to get him killed.

"Why, the sheriff is the ringleader of that bunch. They would have killed me within two weeks," Shipp said.

Although the Reconstruction Era was generally over in Texas, much of Central and West Texas was still ruled by "Mr. Colt," the six-shooter that had been designed by Samuel Colt, the designer and maker of the six-shot revolver that had become the most popular weapon on the frontier. Central Texas, in particular an area including Lampasas, San Saba, Llano, Mills, McCulloch and surrounding counties, was still rife with mob violence and family feuds. Despite a lot of crimes being committed, there were few witnesses willing to step forward and testify either in open court or before a Grand Jury. Besides, the outlaws suspected of the crimes had plenty of friends to provide them with alibis.

It took a vicious murder of a Locker farmer and postmaster named Turner to draw the attention of citizens who were sick of the violence and scared for their own safety, and an election of a young attorney named W. C. Linden from

145

Llano County to shut down the San Saba Mob and to leave a message that no further violence would be tolerated.

Linden, called by many a bright and outstanding lawyer, was seeking the key district attorney's office of the 33rd Judicial District, then known about the state as the "bloody 33rd." In a lengthy interview with San Angelo newspaper reporter Sam Ashburn conducted in his San Antonio office in mid-December 1934, where he had just been appointed Bexar County assistant district attorney, Linden said he fought the old San Saba mob for more than three years.

During that time he received many anonymous letters, was waylaid several times, but was able to "beat them to the draw." Ashburn observed in his story that the feisty attorney was "a fighting man of rich vocabulary and colorful personality."[11]

Linden, who had taken part in more than 200 murder cases during his long courtroom career, was 72 years old when he spent most of a day with Ashburn, recalling the events that took him into San Saba County where he was able to develop a close relationship with Texas Ranger Sergeant W.J.L. Sullivan, who had been sent into the area along with several other rangers to stop the rampant killings that had gripped the area for more than two decades and had claimed more than 50 persons.

Linden's close friendship with Sullivan proved most valuable, he said, particularly since the sheriff who was then serving San Saba County was believed to be controlled by the mob.

According to Sullivan, bushwhackings had gone on for years, not only in San Saba County but in adjoining counties as well. By 1896, so many people had been murdered that the editor of the *San Saba News,* Uluth Mitchell Sanderson, wrote: "This mob work is a disgrace to the county."

Sanderson would later remark that the only thing that kept him alive was the detail of Texas Rangers that had been ordered into the area where they camped on the Colorado River and scouted San Saba and neighboring counties for signs of mob mischief. In addition to the people killed, others were being run off their farms or were moving away to protect their families. Sullivan reported to his superiors that some 50 or more persons had been slain during the violence. It was, indeed, a very bloody time in the Texas Heartland.

Texas Ranger W.J.L. Sullivan who helped break up the San Saba mob. Photo courtesy Mike Cox Collection, Austin, Texas.

The brutal slaying in broad daylight on July 19, 1889, of

James R. Turner, an old, crippled farmer who also was the postmaster of the Knob Ridge post office, drew the ire of law-abiding citizens. Farmer Turner's slaying came only seven days after his oldest son, James H. Turner, 19, was found dead in Willbarger Creek, apparently the victim of accidental drowning. However, many citizens questioned the official ruling in the young man's death because there was "suspicious circumstances" and the man's family believed that "foul play" was involved.[12]

About 2½ months before these incidents occurred, the elder Turner and his wife were getting ready for bed when a bunch of armed horsemen rode up to their home which also housed the Knob Ridge Post Office in one room. The Turner children were in the post office room, either playing or studying. One of the horsemen called out, and one of the older boys went outside to see what the commotion was about. He was asked if his father was home. The boy, realizing trouble was brewing, said "No." He was told that his father had three days to clear out of the county, or the mob would come back and "shoot the hell out of him." The boy's father chose to stay.[13]

A few days later, on an early Sunday morning, Turner's wife heard a ruckus outside among her chickens. She looked out the window and saw three men with guns sneaking about in her chicken yard. Nothing happened that morning; the men being scared away by the clucking hens.

Apparently Turner was being given the warning to leave because he revealed his anti-mob feelings to his neighbor, James F. Daugherty, during a conversation in which Turner said he was tired of the mob violence.

Turner also told Daugherty that he believed that William Madison "Matt" Ford was a member of the mob. Ironically, Ford was also a neighbor of the Turners' and was a cousin of young James R. Turner's wife. He lived about a mile away from the Turner family at Knob Ridge, now the community of

Locker located northwest of San Saba on the road between Richland Springs and Brownwood.[14]

Ford also was a deputy sheriff, serving the Knob Ridge area under then Sheriff S.E.W. Hudson. Ford, called a "bellerin' Methodist," was believed to be a good citizen. However, it was suspected that Postmaster Turner was going through folks mail and passing information he gleaned from the letters to two men who had been run out of the county in 1889. When Daughterly reportedly passed this information on to his neighbor, Ford, became very upset and threatened to break into the post office and kill Turner.[15]

Postmaster Turner was plowing cotton when he was shot and killed in broad daylight on a summer morning on July 19, 1889. Apparently the mob assassins had waited in ambush for Turner to get away from his house before shooting him, a number of times at very close range. The reported distance – said to have been about 300 yards – would later be a part of key testimony when the rangers were able to bring a case to Linden and the grand jury.

According to testimony given by family members who witnessed Turner's murder from the house, three men were seen leaving the farm; the "bellerin' Methodist' Matt Ford, George W. Trowbridge and John W. Harris.[16]

In October 1896, the mob situation appeared to take a change for the better when Rangers turned over a huge pile of evidence and information to the recently elected District Attorney Linden. On October 23, Ford and Trowbridge were indicted by the Grand Jury after hearing more than 300 witnesses.

A motion for a change of venue was made before the court and the case against the two men was moved to Travis County and Austin. The trial began on February 22, 1897.

Albert Burleson, later to become the Postmaster-General of the United States, was then serving as Travis County District Attorney. Linden asked for permission to assist in the prosecution, which was granted.

Ford, who was tried first, had an array of character witnesses appear in his behalf. According to testimony, Ford had sent his sons to finish working the cotton patch after Turner was slain. In addition, Ford was on hand to help make the coffin for the dead farmer's son after the young man was found drowned, and had paid Turner's taxes not long before the murder.[17]

Ford, described as a "praying man" who was concerned for his fellowman, had some well respected friends and neighbors in the community, including the Reverend W. P. Smith, an old fire-and-brimstone Baptist preacher who was said to have been one of Quantrill's raiders, and Aaron Meek, sometimes called Parson Meek, who was then serving as the local justice of the peace and coroner.[18] These men were among many who testified as to the sterling character of Ford.

During testimony, it was brought out that Turner's daughter, Alice, had said during the coroner's inquest that she recognized the men who killed her father and that she could identify Ford and Trowbridge. Turner's wife was reluctant to testify at the inquest, but Daugherty repeated that he had heard Ford state that he "was going to break up the post office and kill Turner." Later, in order to protect themselves from mob vengeance, Alice Turner was influenced by her mother and others to change her testimony.

Ford's defense attorney, the noted trial lawyer James S. Robertson of Austin, raised the question if the daughter could recognize persons 300 or more yards away as they fled the shooting scene. The situation was sticky for Ford because he had a very noticeable hump on his back.

The trial drew statewide interest, and the lawyers really put on a show for spectators and news reporters.

The case's focal point was whether Mrs. Turner and her daughter, Alice, could positively identify Ford and Trowbridge, the alleged shooters, at such a far distance.

"Witness after witness swore it could not be done. Attorney Linden took Travis County Sheriff White over to the courtroom window and pointed out several men coming down the steps of the Capitol, 500 yards away, and White called their names without hesitation," noted Sonnichsen.[19]

Despite the sheriff's testimony and the courtroom demonstration, the defense continued to insist that the women's identification of the men could not be positive.

"How could they help identifying Matt Ford with that buffalo hump on his back?" asked one of the attorneys. "Nobody could be sure," replied the defense.

According to records from that time, the jury was out for a week, but were hung. The vote was 11 for conviction and one for acquittal. The judge discharged them, and ordered a new trial for June. Trowbridge and Ford were released on bond and allowed to go home to San Saba County.

On June 14, 1897, the Ford-Trowbridge murder case was again called for trial with Trowbridge standing before the judge this time.

Again, many witnesses were called and heated arguments echoed through the courthouse as the attorneys squared off. As before in the Ford trial, the jury stayed out for days again while two jurors blocked a conviction. The second trial was nearly a repeat performance of the first. The judge dismissed the jury and the defendants were allowed to go home. Charges against the pair were later dismissed, according to Linden in his interview with San Angelo reporter Sam Ashburn. It was a bitter defeat for the feisty attorney because many at the time believed that Matt Ford was the real leader of the San Saba Mob.

After the Turner killing, Jim Brown, a son of Ace Brown, was assassinated as he returned from church in the China Creek community, Linden recalled. Three men were indicted in Brown's slaying; a man named Bill Ogle was tried in Llano County and given a life sentence in state prison, and another was acquitted. The third man was never brought to trial, Linden said. "In this case a material witness disappeared and was never heard from," he recalled.[20] Through the efforts of Linden, Ogle was later pardoned after the prosecutor had visited him in the penitentiary. Linden told Ashburn in the 1934 interview that he believed that Ogle had been "a weak tool in the hands of other men."[21]

Mob activities faded for about a year after Brown's murder as he left the church gathering.

According to Ashburn's interview with the judge and the notes of historian Sonnichsen, the bushwhacking of Brown "seemed to have the effect of scaring the good people into keeping quiet and the bad ones into leaving or mending their ways."[22] There was no more recorded mob violence until the early part of 1896 when there was two murders committed by mobsters in June.

"In the Locker community, T. A. Henderson and William James were ambushed within a few days of each. They had opened their lips about the mob. Henderson had the regulation nine bullet holes, all fatal. James also died with nine bullet wounds," wrote Ashburn.

T. A. Henderson was killed "up in the post oaks as he was cutting cord wood," Sonnichsen learned. Henderson's wife would later tell Texas Ranger Captain Bill McDonald that her husband had been ordered to leave the county within three days in August 1894, and had done so, relocating to Brownwood. When the Grand Jury met in San Saba later, Henderson returned and testified before that secret body that there were several men in the group that had ordered him to leave without reason. Several of those named were billed and in November 1895 one of them was put on trial. He was acquitted, however, and the other cases were dismissed like so many others brought against mob members.

The same men who Henderson had accused of ordering him out of the country later brought a charge against him of perjury. He was later brought back to San Saba and released on bond. He was awaiting trial when he was shot to death on June 22, 1896.

When killed, Henderson was working with his brother, Fayette, and one of his boys cutting wood for a neighbor who lived two miles north of Richland Springs. Fayette was wounded in the shoulder in the ambush, and he and the boy were able to escape the mob and flee to safety after hiding all night. Fayette Henderson disappeared from the area and the boy went home to report the death of his father.[23]

William James, who lived near Hanna's Crossing on the Colorado River, was murdered about a week later. Although he resided in an area where much of the mob violence occurred, he apparently never had any trouble with the mob. He did talk about the violence, however, at home. One of his children repeated his comments at school and word spread that "he had talked."[24] While hauling a load of water out of the river, he was shot from his wagon as it came out at the crossing. Folks living near the crossing heard the gunfire and went to check on things. James' wagon had blood on one of its wheels. His body, with the mob signature nine bullet holes, was found in the road. Dave Chadwick stayed with the body for most of the day until help could arrive.[25]

In his interview in 1934 with reporter Ashburn, Judge Linden said he had seven men indicted for the deaths of Henderson and James. Although the men were indicted, there was not enough evidence to bring the men to trial.

But the wily district attorney in the frock coat used his so-called ace in the hole. He had the bondsmen for the seven bring them into open court and surrender them. The bondsmen were released and the cases put on the retired docket. He told the seven men that if at the end of six months time he had evidence that they had sold their holdings in the county and had moved out and that no more violence was done in the county that the cases against them would be kept on the docket. If the men did not move and more killings occurred, he would change the venue on the cases, places them in courts all over the state, and if he could not convict them he would break them financially. Nine men were included in the final order. A three-year nightmare was over.[26]

Linden observed that within a year after the suspected mob members had left the county, land values in the San Saba area increased in value three times.

The veteran district attorney said that he believed that "no more than 12 or 15 men" did the killings for the mob, and in another case, he said he developed testimony that 250 witnesses had been run out of the county. He also believed that the mob membership never reached more than 50 or 60, and that none of the men who allegedly did the killings remained in the county.[27]

Linden told reporter Ashburn he had to take the offensive when trying to convict mob members in court. In one trial, Ashburn wrote, the pioneer lawyer "charged into the jury, told them that they did not have the courage to convict a man who had the backing of the mob, that there was no need of his appealing to them, that he knew what the decision would be, that they would acquit the man in a few minutes.

"You fellows will take a walk around the mill pond, kill some poor bumblebee sitting on a broom weed with a blast of tobacco juice and then come back and say the man is free. When you look a mob man in the eye you become a jellyfish, your courage departs, you wilt, you become servants, men in name and cowards at heart."[28]

After scolding the jurymen, Linden turned around to the courtroom, pointed out seven men and declared them members of the mob. He called them by name. He turned to a man whom he described as the chaplain of the group, and said the man was then praying to God that he (Linden) be struck dead for what he was saying.

Linden let everyone in the courtroom know he was not

fearful of any man. Wearing a Prince Albert style frock coat, during his blistering speech the coattail casually opened to reveal a pearl-handled six-shooter tucked into the waistband of his trousers.

When the fiery speech was finished, most in the courtroom expected an acquittal because 11 of the dozen men on the jury had previously acquitted another man whom Linden had accused of being a mobster. The defense attorneys in the case had no argument to make, so the judge gave the case to the jury. Linden decided to go to his hotel room to wait out the jury verdict, so he left the courthouse alone and started across the street. It was a cool April afternoon, he told Ashburn.

Sitting on boxes across from the courthouse were the seven men he singled out as mobsters. Each had his coat on, so Linden knew they were armed and ready. One, Little Jim Ford, had a big knife in his hand. Linden had chastised Ford while he was on the witness stand, saying he was under indictment in another case and had appeared as a witness for another defendant. The lawyer said bitter words were passed among the men and himself.

"Why don't you fellows carry out your plans to kill me? I know you have been shooting men from the shelter of trees so long that you cannot look a man in the eye and pull a trigger. Another thing. You don't know which of you I'm going to kill first but I do, and if you start shooting I will kill three of you before you can get me," he declared.[29]

Friends of Linden soon came up and the seven men left the front porch of the clothing store. The frightened owner had fled the store and left his goods outside all night.

Linden told reporter Ashburn that Dud Barker, then a Texas Ranger who had been sent in to help stop the mob violence, later complained to him that he did not tell him he was about to have trouble. Linden told him it was a job he had to handle himself.

The district attorney, sweating and so tired he could drop,

did not have an opportunity to lay down and rest in his hotel room. A messenger came to tell him that the jury had convicted the defendant.

"It was the most outrageous speech ever made to a jury," Linden said. "I told them that if they did not convict that man that there would come over San Saba a reign of terror that would make Nero's affliction of Rome as peaceful as a kindergarten. I told them that if the man was freed that the time would come when a man would be afraid to whisper their secrets to their own wives at the dead hour of midnight, and that they may as well tear down the courthouse, throw the law books in the river and go back to the beasts. It was the first mob conviction in that county and from that date the mob began to slip and lose ground."[30]

---

[1] Albert Bigelow Paine, <u>Captain Bill McDonald, Texas Ranger</u>, (New York, NY: Little and Ives, 1909) p. 221.

[2] Ibid., p. 222.

[3] Charles L. Sonnichsen, <u>I'll Die Before I Run, The Story of the Great Feuds of Texas</u>, (New York, NY: Harper and Brothers, 1951) p. 165.

[4] W. J. L. Sullivan, <u>Twelve Years in the Saddle with the Texas Rangers</u>, (Lincoln, NE: University of Nebraska Press, 2001) p. 41.

[5] Ibid., p. 41.

[6] C.L. Sonnichsen, Original notes, provided to author by David Johnson.

[7] Ibid.

[8] Ibid.

[9] "Knights of the Golden Circle," <u>The Handbook of Texas Online</u>, <http://www.tshaonline.org/handbook/online/>

[10] Ibid.

[11] Sam Ashburn, San Angelo Morning Times, December 21, 1934.

[12] Ross J. Cox Sr., The Texas Rangers and The San Saba Mob, (San Saba, TX: C&S Farm Press, 2005).

[13] Sonnichsen, Original Notes, op. cit.

[14] The Texas Almanac Sesquicentennial Edition,1857-2007, p. 202.

[15] Cox, op. cit.

[16] Cox, op. cit.

[17] Sonnichsen, Original Notes, op. cit.

[18] Ibid.

[19] Ibid.

[20] Ashburn, op. cit.

[21] Ibid.

[22] Sonnichsen, Original Notes, op. cit.

[23] Sonnichsen, I'll Die Before I Run, The Story of the Great Feuds of Texas, op. cit.

[24] Ibid.

[25] Ibid.

[26] Ashburn, op. cit.

[27] Ibid.

[28] Ibid.

[29] Ibid.

[30] Ibid.

Chapter 17:
The Enforcers

They enforced the law with a heavy hand, but most of all the Texas Rangers were perhaps the defining force for the stabilization and the creation of Texas…the effort put forth in those early days set the foundation for the Texas Rangers that keep Texas safe today.[1]

Stopping mob violence in San Saba County was one of the toughest assignments the noted Frontier Battalion would be given, and the now world famous law enforcement group has quite a history of solving terrible crimes.

According to Ranger reports, lawlessness in San Saba and adjoining counties in Central Texas had been going on for decades. The trouble had accounted for more murders than any other Texas feud – 43 killings eventually being credited to the so-called "San Saba Mob."[2] There were perhaps many more that were unaccounted for.

"Peace and prosperity in San Saba County today bears little resemblance to conditions that once existed here when mob rule held sway, when no man's life was immune from the hazard that the mob council had created," stated a story that appeared in the Thursday, July 24, 1941 issue of *The San Saba Star*.

"Stately hills, majestic groves of trees and sparkling streams that today invite pleasure seekers here are lasting monuments to grim tragedies of bygone days. Many trees designate the exact spot where men gave up their lives at the hands of the mob," the article continued.

The frontier in those days was sparsely settled, there was few to no courts of law to settle the grievances of settlers or to protect their property, thus the people had to take their own measures to keep the peace and to protect themselves from raiders – both Indians and Anglos.

Lawlessness became rampant in the post-Civil War days. Carpetbag government rigged the courts, turned a deaf ear on crime and often terrorized the settlers under the guise of applying the law.[3]

As mob activity flourished, good citizens and businessmen realized that something had to be done to bring peace and order to the county and community.

Judge A. W. Moursund of the 33rd Judicial District Court sent a letter to State Adjutant General W. H. King on December 2, 1889, appealing for help from the Rangers.

"As you are aware several men have been mysteriously killed in the upper part of San Saba County during the last two or three years. The circumstances strongly indicate that there exists an organization which is the cause of these murders and protects each other so that the Grand Jury has been unable to ferret out the perpetrators," he wrote.[4]

Another appeal was sent to Texas Governor Charles A. Culberson for Texas Ranger protection. He immediately ordered that four Rangers be sent to the area to start cleaning up the mobs and arrest other unsavory persons. The four men selected for the job were Edgar T. Neal and Allen Maddox, both of Company E at Alice in deep South Texas, Dudley Barker and Sergeant John H. Sullivan, both of Company B and working at Amarillo.

Sullivan and Barker traveled to Goldthwaite by train and met the other two Rangers on August 13, 1896. The four lawmen then proceeded to San Saba County by horseback accompanied by the Sheriff, S.E.W. Hudson, who had met them in Mills County. They quickly went into camp near Regency, once called Hannah's Crossing, on the Colorado River. It was near this place that rancher William James had been brutally murdered while hauling water from the river to his home nearby. The Rangers would remain at this location for a number of months, quietly gathering information toward making a case or cases against mobsters to be brought before the court.

Sullivan, a veteran Texas Ranger and native Mississippian, was tall, raw-boned and wore a full beard. He looked tough and was tough. In one of his early reports, he wrote:

"The people of both factions, especially the mob element, were antagonistic to us when we first went to San Saba, and our lives were in danger. When we four boys pitched our tent at Hannah's Crossing we shook hands with each other and made a solemn pledge that we would stay there and do our duty if we all had to die together."[5]

Following the arrival of the Rangers, local citizens felt more comfortable about speaking their minds about the violence. A town hall meeting of sorts was called with over 500 people showing up.

Frontier editor U. M. Sanderson of the *San Saba News* took an editorial stance lambasting the mob violence and expressing his full support of the Rangers.

"No man can be a good citizen and encourage by word or action the defiance of law. The Rangers are coming to stay until the lawless element is suppressed," he wrote.

Contrary to reason many San Saba County residents resented the presence of the Rangers. However, quiet-spoken, mild-mannered Edgar T. Neal quickly was able to win their friendship and inspire their trust.

"Neighbors had no way of knowing whether or not his closest neighbor belonged to this secret but notorious mob. Therefore Neal's quiet-spoken manner helped to quell all their jitters," recalled one old-timer in a story by the late Stella Gipson Polk, a Mason County native and accomplished historian.

In her story, Polk stated that Neal was "a loner, and it was a common sight to see him, a solitary horseman, riding out the dim, forgotten trails in the county." In later years, he would be elected sheriff of San Saba County and serve four terms. In his memoirs, Ranger Sgt. Sullivan observed that while the Rangers were passing a group gathered in town, he heard a man inquire "who we were, and another man replied that we were Texas Rangers; whereupon they all laughed, some of them remarking that if we ever got three miles out of town we would never live to get back. We heard the remark but paid no attention to it."[6]

By mid-May 1897, the four Rangers were ready to present their evidence to the Grand Jury.

In their investigation of the Hartman killing, they found evidence enough to arrest a man named Campbell and his two sons, Mick and Dave. According to Sullivan, the men made such conflicting statements in trying to get out of trouble that the Grand Jury indicted Dave Campbell and his father for the murder. Before Dave Campbell could be brought to trial, he jumped bail and fled to Arizona Territory. He was caught seven years later, using the alias "Alex Miller." He was brought back to San Saba for trial, and later acquitted.

"Old man Campbell got a change of venue to Fort Mason, and was convicted and sentenced to seven and a half years in the penitentiary but appealed his case. He was tried 16 times in eight years, and finally got off with a light sentence of two and a half years and went to the penitentiary from Lampasas County," Sullivan wrote.[7] The dead man's father lived long enough to fight the case for eight long years, but he would ultimately spend every dollar he had.

"He sold his farm and home and stock to keep up the prosecution, and when he died at the age of seventy-seven he was renting land. But he had remained faithful to his son to the last," the Ranger recalled.[8]

In the Spring of 1897, a nasty situation developed when Ranger Sullivan and Sheriff Andrew Jackson Hawkins got into a heated argument in the courthouse. Sullivan, frustrated over a mobster being turned loose by a jury despite strong evidence, pulled his pistol on the newly elected sheriff.

Hawkins was believed to be a mob sympathizer if not a secretive member so Sullivan had no respect for the man. Before the argument could get out of hand, another Ranger stopped the incident from getting worse. As a result of the courthouse dispute, the district judge ordered the Rangers from the building and wrote Adjutant General Mabry seeking Sullivan's removal.

San Saba County Sheriff A. J. Hawkins while serving in office. Note pistol grip in waistband beneath coat. Photo courtesy Hawkins descendent Jack Siscoe.

The feisty Sullivan, apparently under much stress, had started to drink heavily. He was found on several occasions in

San Saba saloons drinking with known mob members and several times had to be helped back to camp. Sullivan's superior, Captain Bill McDonald, cautioned the Ranger that he needed to stop his drinking and improve his behavior. On May 4, 1897, McDonald came to San Saba and took personal charge of the Ranger detachment. He was accompanied by another Ranger from his company. There were now eight Rangers working the immediate area, not only seeking evidence against the ever-present mob, but also catching cattle rustlers, horse thieves and wanted fugitives.

Joining the San Saba detachment were Van Lane, Billy McCaully, Ed Donnelly, Bob McClure, George Thomas, Jack Harley, Doc Neely and Eugene "Blue" Bell.

Although McDonald made an immediate move to strengthen the Rangers' presence by moving his camp within a mile of San Saba, there were some people that still tried to curtail the Rangers efforts to end violence and bloodshed. On January 9, 1898, McDonald received the following letter, as it was written:

"Sur, I will rite you a note to let you no we have tuck all the abuse and damned foolishness off of you that we are goin too and if you don't leave San Saba co we will fill you so full of led it will take a frait train to hall you to the grave yard. You have bloed about enuff we are not afrade of you or your Rangers or big headed Charlie Culberson (the governor) you cant convic our men the state pays our way it don't cost nothing to git lawyers the state funsh the munny to hyer them with, you had (better) take your damnd out fit and leave or you will regret hit this is your last warnin we mean busness and after you are gon we will not live a single anty mob man in the county we will kill hole shootin match. Your Mob."[9]

Ranger Edgar Neal proved his worth to McDonald when he came to the captain's bedside late Sunday night and woke him up.

"I've got a hunch Bill Ogle is going to make a run for it. If he gets the jump on us he's got the whole West to lose himself in. We may never find him," Neal said. It was the night before court was to convene on Monday.[10]

The groggy McDonald told Neal: "Whatever you decide go ahead and do it."

Neal rode in the night to Ogle's home and found a place at the base of a hill where he could watch the skyline. Just before daylight Ogle came riding down the hill. Neal surprised Ogle, disarmed him and put the man in handcuffs. It was suspected that Ogle was the leader of the mob and was the triggerman that killed Jim Brown some four years earlier.[11] No one ever expected that Ogle would be arrested.

When the San Saba County Court convened, Judge Allison was fearful that more violence could be expected so he had Ranger Captain McDonald to post his Rangers around the courthouse square. The quiet, unassuming Neal was put in the courtroom proper, armed with two Colt pistols and a Winchester rifle. Although the judge had a pistol beneath his coat, he told Neal to get rid of the rifle.

"Judge, the State of Texas pays me to carry this Winchester. With the court's permission I shall continue to carry it. And sir, it is fully loaded," Neal replied.[12]

The presence of so many Rangers at the courthouse brought reassurance to the crowded courtroom.

Confederate Army Captain W. H. Ledbetter took the witness chair. A new surge of courage came to the spectators because the former rebel officer was fearless and very well respected in the county. The crowd strained to hear his every word as Ledbetter told of the suffering and abuse he had received from the mob. According to court records, witness after witness voluntarily followed the old veteran to tell their stories of mob action. More than 300 testified.

There are a lot of stories now recorded. For many years they were only whispered among those that the storyteller could trust.

Moses Brazil came to San Saba in 1875 and settled on Cherokee Creek in the Chappel community. He later recalled that he had once come upon mobsters butchering a neighbor's cow. On seeing Brazil, the mob made his life miserable. Once the mob set fire to his rail fence and it burned to the log cribs before being discovered. Other times, in an attempt to get his wife, Martha, out of the house when she was alone, the mob would drag chains across the porch, flash lanterns from different directions and do other things to frighten her. Finally, the mob told her they were going to burn her house but did not want to harm she and the children. The mob left when she banished a gun and threatened to shoot to kill. Soon, neighbors and friends banded together to stop mob violence in the community.[13]

The arrest of Bill Ogle on August 26, 1897, by Ranger Edgar Neal and Ogle's subsequent trial in neighboring Llano County, helped Captain McDonald and his special Ranger unit to finally succeed in bringing an end to mob violence. Ogle, a key figure in the mob, was found guilty of killing Jim Brown some four years earlier when he was shot off his horse while leaving a church meeting. Brown's wife also was wounded in the ambush. Ogle got a life sentence in state prison.

The Rangers also made a positive impression on mob members and other lawbreakers that violence in San Saba and adjoining counties would not be tolerated. Proof of this was illustrated when Ranger Dud Barker was confronted outside the courthouse by James Boren, a suspected mob member armed with a rifle and encouraged by plenty of liquor. When Boren accosted Barker, the Ranger attempted to arrest him. Boren resisted, however, and Barker shot the man dead.[14] The incident happened on November 3, 1898.

For many years, there was a boot track imprinted in the concrete walkway at the west entrance to the county courthouse. It was put there in whimsy by Edgar Neal when the sidewalk was being laid sometime in the 1920s. Its proximity to the courthouse was fitting because it was there that Neal made one of his typically heroic stands in face of danger. It is a small boot track because Neal had small feet, despite weighing about 225 pounds.

Neal was standing guard at the courthouse with Dud Barker on the day that Barker shot Boren. Neal and Barker gave the mobsters "two minutes to get out of San Saba."[15]

Although the Rangers were quick to make examples of frontier justice, both Captain McDonald and Sergeant Sullivan reported later that what ultimately made San Saba County safe was that eight former Rangers met and married local women and settled in the county. One of them, Edgar Neal, was elected sheriff and served for 16 years. Barker later served a number of years as sheriff of Pecos County in West Texas.

Ironically, Ogle, the only man ever convicted of any of the San Saba Mob murders, was later pardoned by Governor Thomas M. Campbell after serving 10 years of his life sentence. Ogle lived in Runnels County after being released from prison. Later, he moved to Wichita Falls where he went to work as a city policeman. He worked as a city lawman until a short time before his death in 1934.

---

[1] Mike Cox, The Texas Rangers, Wearing the Cinco Peso 1821-1900, Vol. 1, (New York, NY: Forge Books, 2008).

[2] Ibid.

[3] "San Saba Mob – A Saga of the Past," San Saba News and Star, May 1, 1975.

[4] C.L. Sonnichsen, Original notes, provided to author by David Johnson.

[5] W. J. L. Sullivan, Twelve Years in the Saddle for Law and Order on the Frontiers of Texas, (Austin, TX: Von Boeckmann-Jones, 1909).

[6] Ibid.

[7] Ibid.

[8] Ibid.

[9] The Richland Springs Eye-Witness, December 10, 1959.

[10] San Saba Mob, op. cit.

[11] Ibid.

[12] Ibid.

[13] San Saba County Historical Commission, San Saba County History, 1856-1983, (San Saba, TX: San Saba County Historical Commission, 1983) p. 37.

[14] Cox, op. cit.

[15] Irene Gibson, San Angelo Standard-Times, July 16, 1967.

Epilogue:
They Never Learn

After the turn of the century, the bloody 1880s and 1890s became rather peaceful. With so many former Texas Rangers being elected as sheriffs or serving as deputies or town marshals, criminal activities was reduced to "sometime murders" along with lots of barroom brawls, domestic disputes, bootlegging and arguments over ownership of livestock.

Yet, the region still had cattle rustlers and horse thieves, especially when times got hard. Despite many being sent to prison or county jail terms, thievery still existed. Even into the Great Depression years.

Between April 24, 1935, and July 17, 1935, Cecil Gatlin trucked to the Fort Worth Stockyards from San Saba County 79 head of cattle, including 32 calves, mostly unbranded, and some cows that were unbranded. The first shipment was sold in the name of Cecil Gatlin and the remaining animals were sold under the name of Mrs. C.A. Thompson, who called Pontotoc in Mason County as her home address.[1]

An investigation into missing livestock from some six ranches in San Saba County led to Gatlin's arrest. He was indicted by the Grand Jury on 10 counts of livestock theft, and Mrs. Thompson also was indicted in connection with these same thefts. Lawmen soon learned that Mrs. Thompson was actually Gatlin's wife, Mrs. Annabel Lee Gatlin, and that Cecil Gatlin was a minister of Christian Churches in Richland Springs, Rochelle and Menard.

In addition to the San Saba Grand Jury indictments, the Gatlins also had been previously indicted in Menard County, charged with horse stealing.[2]

Cecil Gatlin, when arraigned, pleaded guilty to three charges of horse stealing and received a sentence of four years in each case, the sentences to run concurrently. The horse theft indictments against Mrs. Gatlin were continued as were the cattle rustling charges and other indictments in San Saba County until the Spring terms of the district court of Menard and San Saba counties.

Gatlin's trial was postponed until November 7 because a jury was unavailable at the time. In seeking a continuance in the cattle stealing cases, Gatlin claimed that he had bought the cattle from a young man, who was then deceased. When no bill of sale was presented, the prosecuting attorney took issue with his claim. When the judge overruled his claim, Gatlin decided to plead guilty and waived the selection of a jury.

The owners of the stolen cattle and the alleged number of head taken included A.N. Oglesby, 6 head; J.M. Owens, 2 head; Leonard Smith, 1; D.S. Smith, 1; J. T. McConnell, 4 head; G. W. Gray, 62 head; Ward Holman, one horse; and C.C. Taylor, one washing machine.

According to the report in the *Cattleman Magazine,* association brand inspectors Cecil Rourk and Sam McAulay furnished vital testimony in the cases, thus causing Gatlin to plead guilty. However, Mrs. Gatlin's cases were postponed for an indefinite period because she had voluntarily entered the Southwestern Hospital for the Insane at San Antonio for observation. The hospital's assistant director, a Dr. Johnson, was in attendance at the trial when the guilty pleas were entered by her husband.[3]

Those taking part in the prosecution of the cases were County Attorney Dick Johnson and Sheriff Will Doran, both of San Saba, and District Attorney Carlos Ashley of Llano and Menard County Sheriff Cecil Walston.

The cattle raisers' association was organized mainly for the purpose of catching cattle rustlers and horse thieves. The cases were brought about on evidence developed by the association's brand inspectors working at the Fort Worth market, then the second largest in the country and the largest in the southwest.

In another case that originated in San Saba County, Porter Pearcy was charged with the embezzlement of cattle from the Sloan Sisters Ranch. Pearcy was tried in San Saba County, but the trial ended with a hung jury. Pearcy was the foreman of the Sloan Sisters Ranch and with the exception of being away one year while serving in the Army in World War I, he had never worked on any other place.

Despite earlier frontier justice and later, good investigation work, thieves seem to never learn that "Crime Does Not Pay."

---

[1] The Cattleman Magazine, September 1935, published by the Texas and Southwestern Cattle Raisers Association, Fort Worth.

[2] Ibid.

[3] Ibid.

Bibliography

Unpublished Material

Hannah, Archie Douglas. Memoirs. 1958. Frederica B. Wyatt, Kimble County Historical Commission, Junction.

Books

Barr, Michael. *Rope Burns & Lead Poisoning, The Wild West in Central Texas*. Gatesville, TX: MikesBooks, 2006.

Barler, Miles. *Early Days In Llano, Personal Reminiscences*. Privately published.

Banta, Eugene Mardell. *20 Years A Buckaroo*. Ozark, Mo.: Dogwood Printing Company, 2007.

Blackwell, Hartal Langford. *Mills County - The Way It Was*. Goldthwaite, TX: The Eagle Press, 1976.

Bowles, Flora Gatlin. *A No Man's Land Becomes A County*. Goldthwaite, TX: The Eagle Press, 1958.

Burton, Jeffrey. *The Deadliest Outlaws*. Portsmouth, England. Palomino Books, 2007.

Carlson, Paul H. *Texas Woollybacks, The Range Sheep and Goat Industry*. College Station, TX: Texas A&M University Press, 1982.

Cook, Donna Gholson. *Gholson Road, Revolutionaries and Texas Rangers*. Bloomington, Ind.: 1st Books Library, 2004.

Cox, Mike. *The Texas Rangers, Wearing the Cinco Peso, 1821-1900*. New York: A Tom Doherty Associates Book, 2008.

Cox, Ross J., Sr. *The Texas Rangers and the San Saba Mob*. San Saba, TX: C&S Farm Press, 2005.

Conner, John E., selections by Katherine S. Conner. *A Great While Ago.* Austin: Eakin Publications Inc. 1983.

DeArment, Robert K. *Deadly Dozen, Twelve Forgotten Gunfighters of the Old West.* Norman, Ok.: University of Oklahoma Press, 2003.

Eckhardt, C.F. *Tales of Bad Men, Bad Women and Bad Places.* Lubbock: Texas Tech University Press, 1999.

Elzner, Jonnie Ross. *Relighting Lamplights of Lampasas County, Texas.* Hill Country Press, 1974.

Fisher, O.C. *It Occurred In Kimble: The Story of A Texas County.* Houston: Anson Jones Press, 1937.

Hall, Sarah Harkey. *Surviving on the Texas Frontier: The Journal of an Orphan Girl in San Saba County.* Austin. Eakin Press. 1996.

Hamrick, Alma Ward. *The Call Of The San Saba, A History of San Saba County.* San Antonio: The Naylor Company, 1941.

Harkey, Dee. *Mean As Hell.* Albuquerque: University of New Mexico Press, 1948.

Havins, T.R. *Something About Brown: A History of Brown County, Texas.* Brownwood, TX: Banner Printing Company. 1958.

Johnson, David. *John Ringo, King of the Cowboys, His Life and Times.* Denton, TX: The University of North Texas Press, 2008.

King, Irene Marschall. *John O. Meusebach, German Colonizer In Texas.* Austin: University of Texas Press, 1967.

Lampasas County Historical Commission. *Lampasas County Texas: Its History and Its People.* Marceline, Mo.: Walsworth Publishing Company, 1991.

McCallum, Henry D. and Frances T. *The Wire That Fenced The West.* Norman, Ok.: University of Oklahoma Press, 1965.

McSwain, Robert J. Jr. *The Blue and Grey, Perry County, Mississippi's Civil War Soldiers.* Carrollton, Ms.: Pioneer Publishing Company, 2006.

Metz, Leon Claire. *The Shooters, A Gallery of Notorious Gunmen from the American West.* New York: Berkley Books, 1996.

Moursund, John Stribling. *A Blanco County History.* Publisher unknown.

Nolan, Frederick, *Tascosa, Its Life and Gaudy Times.* Lubbock, TX: Texas Tech University Press, 2007.

O'Neal, Bill. *Cattlemen vs. Sheepherders, Five Decades of Violence in the West.* Austin, TX: Eakin Press, 1989.

-------------- *Encyclopedia of Western Gunfighters.* Norman, Ok.: University of Oklahoma Press, 1979.

-------------- *The Bloody Legacy of Pink Higgins.* Austin: Eakin Press. 1999.

San Saba County Historical Commission. *San Saba County History, 1856- 1983.* San Saba, TX: 1983.

Sloan, Jym A. *Old Timers Of Wallace Creek.* San Saba, TX: The San Saba News, 1958.

Smith, David Paul. *Frontier Defense in the Civil War, Texas' Rangers and Rebels.* College Station, TX: Texas A&M University Press, 1992.

Smith, Tevis Clyde. *Frontier's Generation, A Pioneer History Of Brown County With Sidelights On The Surrounding Territory.* Brownwood, TX : Greenwood Press, 1931.

Sonnichsen, C.L. *I'll Die Before I Run, The Story of the Great Feuds in Texas.* New York. Harper and Brothers Publishers, 1951.

Southwestern Historical Quarterly, Volume XLIV, July 1940- April 1941, Austin: Texas State Historical Association, 1941.

Spiller, Wayne, compiler. *Handbook Of McCulloch County History, Vol.II.*
Staked Plains Press, 1984.

Spence, Ruth Griffin. *The Nice and Nasty of Brown County, A Collection of Stories*. Brownwood, TX: Banner Printing Company.

Stephens, Robert W. *Mannen Clements, Texas Gunfighter*. Dallas: Private Printing, 1996.

Paine, Albert Bigelow. *Captain Bill McDonald, Texas Ranger*. New York. Little and Ives, 1909.

Wharton, Clarence R. *Texas Under Many Flags*. Publisher Unknown. 1930.

Yadon, Laurence J. with Dan Anderson. *200 Texas Outlaws and Lawmen, 1835-1935*. Gretna, La.: Pelican Publishing Company, 2008.

Periodicals
(Newspapers and Magazines)

Enchanted Rock Magazine
The Cattleman Magazine
True West Magazine
Texas Rangers Dispatch Magazine
WOLA Journal
West Texas Historical Association Year Books, 1950, 2006
The Dallas Morning News
Fort Worth Star-Telegram
The Graham Leader
Richland Springs Eye-Witness
San Saba News and Star
San Angelo Standard-Times
San Antonio Express

Websites

American Life Histories: Manuscripts from the Federal Writers' Project, 1936-1940.

Handbook of Texas Online: Texas State Historical Association,
   Austin.
Texashistory: textiles.com